Praise for *Built to Last*

"Mike Murphy offers a wise blending of research on educational change with the insights and experiences of a veteran educator. This book is conceptually rich and actionably practical."

—Jay McTighe
Author of the *Understanding by Design*® series and
Leading Modern Learning

"When a district or school change effort does 'take root,' what was present for this to happen during the evolving cycles to sustainable change is the million-dollar question. Michael Murphy is really onto something in this book as he brings to life the types of conditions, the necessary mechanics, and the relationship structures that, when cultivated during the lifespan of a change effort, propel the change to endure for the long haul."

—Lisa Guzzardo Asaro, EdS
Macomb ISD (Michigan) School Improvement Consultant

"Murphy's book *Built to Last: The School Leader's Guide for Sustaining Change While Managing Resistance* is a wonderfully written, well-organized must-read for school leaders who want to be effective in leading change in their district or school. What makes the book especially helpful is the clear message of what leaders can do specifically to assist teachers to adapt new initiatives in a way that maximizes the impact on their students' learning. Readers will enjoy the conversational writing style and practical illustrations of the author's experiences as he explores the stages of change: Initiation, Implementation, and Institutionalization. Overall, Murphy not only provides important, timely, well-researched information but also offers hope and encouragement that our past efforts to lead change do not have to define us. His message suggests we are all learners and inspires us to adapt new ways of doing business that elevate all of us as educators to have a more lasting impact on our work."

—Marcia Imbeau
Professor, Department of Curriculum and Instruction
University of Arkansas

"This book is definitely one I wish was available when I was a building principal. It unpacks the concepts of 'sustained' change and 'effectively-managed resistance' in ways few others have. I appreciated the practical district-based examples, clear strategies presented in ways that make them easy to implement, and the connections to research- and evidenced-based approaches. Plan to use your highlighter and sticky notes quite a bit in this must-read text!"

—Frederick Brown
Chief Learning Office/Deputy, Learning Forward

"As leaders, we all experience the challenges that accompany change. In *Built to Last*, Mike Murphy provides well-crafted essential actions and myriad tools for listening, addressing resistance, and conducting constructive conversations to support leaders as they navigate change for their organization."

—Jana Burns
Deputy Executive Director, Region 10 Educational
Service Center (TX)

"Mike Murphy has seamlessly put together personal narrative, case studies, 'macro' learning on change management, and 'micro' strategies for on-the-ground change all in one place! It is a tour de force, actually helping readers learn big ideas in change management and smaller, more specific skills for 'in-the-moment' conversations. A great addition to a school leader's bookshelf."

—Jennifer Abrams
Communications Consultant and Author
Having Hard Conversations and
Hard Conversations Unpacked: The Whos, the Whens, and the What Ifs

"The book thoroughly discusses the key concept of resistance, how to manage it, the ramifications of not managing it effectively, and the reasons why resistance occurs in the first place. This is a fundamental and valuable feature that sets this book apart."

—Karen Tichy
Assistant Professor of Educational Leadership, Saint Louis University
St. Louis, MO

"For any school leader seeking a blueprint for successful change management and long-term success, you've found it. This is both a practical guide and a replicable approach for leading through shifting priorities while truly improving outcomes for students."

—Martha Moore
Senior Director of Educator Effectiveness
Tennessee Department of Education

"Once again Michael Murphy has brought us that special combination of head and heart so desperately needed in educational administration. Any leader struggling with how to improve outcomes for students and staff MUST read this book. Your resulting commitment to the work and belief that it can be done will be brought back to life with renewed energy."

—Cora Stempel
Deputy Superintendent
Dutchess County BOCES (NY)

Built to Last

The School Leader's Guide for Sustaining Change While Managing Resistance

Michael Murphy

Foreword by Carol Ann Tomlinson

FOR INFORMATION:

Corwin
A SAGE Companyy
2455 Teller Road
Thousand Oaks, California 91320
(800) 233-9936
www.corwin.com

SAGE Publications Ltd.
1 Oliver's Yard
55 City Road
London EC1Y 1SP
United Kingdom

SAGE Publications India Pvt. Ltd.
B 1/I 1 Mohan Cooperative Industrial Area
Mathura Road, New Delhi 110 044
India

SAGE Publications Asia-Pacific Pte. Ltd.
18 Cross Street #10-10/11/12
China Square Central
Singapore 048423

Publisher: Arnis Burvikovs
Development Editor: Desirée A. Bartlett
Acquisitions Editor: Ariel Curry
Editorial Assistant: Caroline Timmings
Production Editor: Natasha Tiwari
Copy Editor: Terri Lee Paulsen
Typesetter: Hurix Digital
Proofreader: Barbara Coster
Indexer: Integra
Cover Designer: Candice Harman
Marketing Manager: Sharon Pendergast

Printed in the United States of America

Library of Congress Cataloging-in-Publication Data

Names: Murphy, Michael, author.

Title: Built to last: the school leader's guide for sustaining change while managing resistance / Michael Murphy.

Description: First edition. | Los Angeles : Corwin Press, Inc, [2021] | Includes bibliographical references.

Identifiers: LCCN 2020025095 | ISBN 9781544387451 (paperback) | ISBN 9781544387499 (epub) | ISBN 9781544387482 (epub) | ISBN 9781544387475 (ebook)

Subjects: LCSH: Educational change. | Educational leadership. | Education—Aims and objectives.

Classification: LCC LB2806 .M858 2021 | DDC 371.2—dc23

LC record available at https://lccn.loc.gov/2020025095

This book is printed on acid-free paper.

20 21 22 23 24 10 9 8 7 6 5 4 3 2 1

Table of Contents

Foreword

In a 50-year career in education, I have partnered with, observed, and been "subject to" many and varied educational leaders. Some have inspired me and magnified my work. Some have depleted my reserves and made me question my relevance. Along the way, I have inadvertently become a student of leaders and leadership. I am convinced of two actualities: (1) Leaders are the only real hope we have for remaking our schools into what they need to be to effectively serve each student in their care, and (2) leaders who ultimately catalyze others to create that degree of positive change in a school are rare indeed.

Despite great differences in personality, knowledge base, and approach to leading, leaders with whom I have worked or with whom I studied who made a profound and long-lasting difference in the direction of a school and the prospects of its people seemed to me to share at least four common traits.

Vision

These leaders succeeded because they couldn't do otherwise. They were burdened by a realization that the organization they led could not continue in its present direction without harming children and faculty who were at their mercy. The changes they sought were not small, incremental ones. They sought to reinvent culture and practice. They were convinced to the bone that not to change radically was to do lasting harm—or at the very least, they believed an admonition by Edwin Land, inventor, scientist, and founder of the Polaroid Corporation, that for all of us, "Not to change, is to die." On the positive side, their vision was fueled by a conviction that they and their colleagues were fully capable of making the changes necessary to chart a better course. They had a vision for a better future and could also articulate it clearly to others so it became a shared vision and could fuel the energies of all those on the front lines of change.

Empathy

These leaders were empathetic. Their degree of interpersonal skills varied, but they all sought to see the world through the eyes of the young people their organization served and the eyes of the people they asked to join them in making deep change. Because of their empathy for students of very diverse backgrounds, they listened to those students and were continually moved to improve the prospects of those young people through changing school practice and culture. Because of their empathy for faculty, they listened to faculty and sought to support them in a range of ways that were meaningful to the teachers so that the change process was cushioned a bit and so that teachers felt increasingly confident of their capacity to make the changes they sought to make. Their empathy created a foundation for trust building with faculty, students, and parents.

Focus

In the face of incessant demands on their time from every hand, these leaders did not lose focus on the change they felt compelled to lead. They were consistently in classrooms to learn with and from teachers. They ensured that faculty gatherings focused on learning in order to continue to grow the change, on sharing stories about successes and questions about missteps, and on assessing their shared direction. These leaders ensured that all professional learning was relevant to the change. They consistently celebrated meaningful progress. They consistently invited and responded to feedback. Their focus made it possible for teachers to focus.

Resilience

Along the way, when teachers, parents, or community members got anxious or angry, the leaders listened, reflected on what they were hearing, learned from it, and moved forward. In most instances, the forward movement was informed in some way by the sentiments of stakeholders. While they themselves were sometimes frustrated, discouraged, or angry, they revisited the vision, drew on their ability to see the world through the eyes of others, and sought ways to buoy themselves and to encourage optimism and continuing growth in those involved in the change.

I've seen leaders who had the vision but who got lost because they failed to make it a group vision. I've seen leaders who had the vision but got sidetracked daily by the demands on their time, losing focus until the vision gradually dissipated and finally disappeared. I've seen leaders who had great focus but lacked empathy, causing others to feel that the change was all about the leader—to "polish" his image, or to further her promotion possibilities. And I've seen leaders who had a vision, empathy, and focus but who were easily scared away from the vision by the anger or vitriol of some stakeholders. It's difficult to nurture all four traits, it seems.

Even the leaders whom I've seen make remarkable and lasting change and whom I have come to hold in high regard struggled at times during the long years it takes to work alongside others to remake schools. And this is the punch line of this foreword for *Built to Last*. In my sample of leaders to emulate, none had a deep understanding of the change process, its stages, and the significance of it and teacher needs during those stages. None of them had a ready repertoire of responses to pushback. The difficult journeys they guided would have been less fraught with tension had they had an opportunity to learn from a book like this one before they undertook the change or as they persisted through it.

I've had the great privilege of writing and presenting with Mike Murphy over the last 10 years. I am struck over and over by the eagerness with which school leaders listen as he shares with them the knowledge and wisdom he has garnered from his long career as an educational leader. I hear in their comments, "I-wish-I-had-known-that" reflections. I see "aha!" moments in their eyes as they learn. And I understand all those responses because I always share those feelings when I'm learning from him.

As Mike says in the first pages of this book, he has never known a principal or other school leader who didn't want to do a good job. I believe that many leaders whose heads and hearts are in the right place could become the successful agents of school change with the kind of guidance, support, and experiential wisdom that is in the pages of this book. For me, that's cause for optimism!

Carol Ann Tomlinson, EdD
William Clay Parrish, Jr. Professor Emeritus
School of Education and Human Development
University of Virginia

Acknowledgments

This book has felt somewhat like a culmination of thoughts, ideas, strategies, tips, and conversations that I am eager to share with you. Unlike other manuscripts I have written, this particular one rather smoothly "flowed" out of my head and onto the paper. Now, that may or may not be a good thing, depending on what you think of my mind; nevertheless, the "flow" that I felt was out of a sense that all of what we have known about school improvement and working with people is inextricably connected and forms a clear and whole picture of action for all of us as we work to make things better for teachers and students.

In so many ways, this work carries the voices of others who have influenced my world and my thinking:

- My wife, who never ceases to amaze me with her smart, steady, calming support of my highs, my frustrations, and my relentless (and perhaps aggravating) focus;

- My daughter, son, and their amazing families, who remind me every day how fatherhood and grandfatherhood are both a challenge and a blessing;

- Carol Ann Tomlinson, who in her quiet, brilliantly conceived way challenges my thinking while sending me a clear message that she cares about my soul;

- My great pals in San Antonio, where I only lived for four years but developed such strong relationships that I can't imagine living as far away from them as I now do;

- Educational leaders and friends who have shaped my thinking, including Michael Fullan, Shirley Hord, Stephanie Hirsh, Gerald Ponder, Betty Ann Fults, Robbie Mitchell, Sonia Caus Gleason, Glenn Singleton, and many more;

- All of the various school leaders and school district leaders I have worked with who take up the banner each day, strive to do well, and care about making things better;
- The seven folks from our two case study districts who were so forthcoming and intuitive during our interviews; and
- Ariel Curry, Caroline Timmings, Natasha Tiwari, Terri Lee Paulsen, and all of the folks at Corwin Press, who were so helpful and creative.

When you've been on this earth for 68 years, you amass quite a lot of living. My life continues to be a varied quilt of my faith and the people and experiences that are still defining me and my work. For all of these reasons, I am blessed.

PUBLISHER'S ACKNOWLEDGMENTS

Corwin gratefully acknowledges the contributions of the following individuals:

Angela M. Mosley, Professor
John Tyler Community College
Henrico, VA

LaQuita Outlaw, Principal
Bay Shore Middle School
Bay Shore, NY

Karen L. Tichy, Assistant Professor of Educational Leadership
Saint Louis University
St. Louis, MO

About the Author

Dr. Michael Murphy is a national leadership coach, trainer, planning facilitator, and consultant. Even though he is a native Texan, he is now delighted to live in the Boston, Massachusetts area so he can be close to some of his family. He draws from 44 years of educational experience in urban, suburban, and rural school district settings as he trains and works with instructional coaches, teacher leaders, school leaders, and district leaders both internationally and across North America. Much of Michael's work supports school and district leaders in planning and implementing large-scale improvement initiatives, differentiated instructional practices, the design and implementation of instructional coaching systems, visioning, understanding change and its effect on people, evaluating school improvement progress, designing exceptional professional learning, and facilitating learning in how to engage people in productive, relationship-rich, results-based conversations. Since 2009, he has consulted with varieties of school leaders in 19 states and two Canadian provinces and has presented in numerous state, national, and international symposia and conferences.

Michael's personal public-school experiences include his work as teacher, elementary specialist, assistant principal, principal, director of planning and evaluation, special assistant to the superintendent, assistant superintendent, and acting superintendent, all in several Dallas/Ft. Worth area (TX) school districts. He holds a bachelor of fine arts degree and a master's degree in elementary education from Texas Tech University and a doctorate degree in curriculum and instruction and school leadership from the University of North Texas. He has published numerous articles for national and international journals and is a contributing author or lead author for six educational books in the last 10 years.

Michael lives with his wife of 44 years and enjoys numerous interests when not coaching, training, or consulting. These interests include the production of various forms of art media, golf, working out, travel, and being with his family. Michael can be reached at mmurphy170@gmail.com.

Introduction

The Reality

I'm a worrier. So, I wrote this book for fellow worriers—school leaders who live each day on the edge, wondering how to make life better for their teachers, staff, and students. This is a book for those individuals willing to examine their own practices as well as working to change the conditions for others. This book is for those leaders who are willing to change their behavior on behalf of those who inhabit the walls with them.

There is good reason for my worries and for this book. Most of us don't usually feel as though we are getting lasting results in our schools. Contributing to this is the feeling that we are often participants in a frenzy of poorly led and managed school improvements. Living and working in schools these days feels, to a lot of us, like existing in this whirlwind of well-intentioned actions, erratic reactions, quick fixes, and scattered attempts. Teachers do their best to address the moment-to-moment challenges that they face each day while attempting to cultivate great working exchanges with their colleagues and remain focused on the goals for both their own professional learning and their students' learning. School leaders do their best to spend each day not only putting out massive fires and tiny irritations but also find themselves participating in endless meetings, encouraging their coworkers, cheerleading, correcting, and counseling. School specialists such as instructional coaches live in the netherworld of the "in between": not really knowing if they have any authority while desperately wishing they could simultaneously build relationships with teachers and demand changes in the short amount of time they have with them.

In other words, life in schools is like being in a persistent, sometimes rancorous whirlwind of change. Because of the sheer magnitude of what we are often asked to address, that whirlwind sometimes feels more like a blender. And the cuts hurt us and the people with whom we work.

Now, nothing I have said yet is particularly new to us. We have been living in this "change blender" for quite a while, trying to practice a new understanding of curriculum and instruction, deal with rough conditions, and meet challenging demands from a variety of sources. Book after book has been written about change and how to lead and manage change. Author after author has published his or her own "recipe" for change, encouraging all of us to simply follow their checklists for ultimate satisfaction and success. Simultaneously, teachers have been exposed to dramatic curriculum upheavals and impressively dumbing amounts of training to ensure that their new curriculum knowledge will translate to more effective instruction. Instructional coaching programs have sprouted like new seedlings in the garden—without any intentionality of thinking through what these instructional coaching programs are to accomplish, who the targets of their coaching are, and how to determine coaching success. These are big efforts and yet, many of our schools remain unchanged. Thus, we continue to search for "the answer" or a specific program to meet the particular contextual issues we face. Just as quickly as we latch onto a "solution," we abandon it when realizing its inadequacies and blame it on factors out of our control. And just as the ingredients in the blender, we feel jostled, cut, and minimized, each of us becoming so small and unrecognizable that we lose our own identity and our individual desire for relevance and joy in our workplaces.

So, what are the contributing reasons for the continued lack of consistent progress, the degree of personal dissatisfaction that exists among teachers, and the perpetual exploration of quick fixes that yield no sustained durability? The culprit may be living right with us—in other words, we may be reaping what we sow. Have these overwhelming whirlwind conditions and our own desire for fast relief focused us slowly but steadily on exactly the things that don't work? Are we as leaders often feeling compelled to act in unfocused ways, reacting to issues rather than responding to them? Are we seeing resistance to the changes for good reasons? Is the press for quick improvement actually sending a dangerous message that quick improvement is possible and can be sustained in a variety of schools and contexts?

The Good News

The good news is that as we attempt to help schools become better places for teachers and students, there is hope in terms of strategic efforts and school operations that lead these places to lasting, enduring improvements. We *can* build changes in schools that will last by ensuring steady progress over time. We have quite a bit of knowledge and practical understanding that quick fixes essentially do not work over the years. As the *Harvard Business Review* ("Re-evaluating Incremental Innovation," 2018) reminds us, there is power in incremental improvement—the kind of improvement that capitalizes on small but focused improvements and builds in a steady and clear direction, understood with clarity by all doing the work. This brand of incremental improvement, while seeming foreign to most of us weathering the demand for quick change, tends to lead toward the stable, deepening development of practices that impact students.

There is also hope that this method of strategizing actions and operating schools can, at the same time, build and enable relationships among students and among adults that will create joy, passion, and effective focus, aimed at creating the type of community in schools which promotes achievement. This hope is grounded in simple human nature. I have never seen a principal or teacher who did not want to be successful. I find that teachers and principals will generally work hard for the improvements we need if a few conditions are present where they work. I think that you can press for better student results as you work toward more powerful relationships among the adults doing such important work (in other words, I do not think that you have to sacrifice one for the other). Most resistance to our efforts that we see and feel comes from a place of confusion about the goal or a lack of trust in either the leader, the work, or each other.

What This Book Will Not Be

This book will not just focus on change principles; instead, each chapter will be focused on the developmental construction of changes that will last. I'll focus on the phases of change and then address highly important leadership practices that will simultaneously move the change forward and address the kinds of resistance that may appear during that phase of the work. The subtitle of this work mentions "sustaining change while managing resistance." I won't treat those two topics separately. I believe that effective long-term leadership will reduce resistance and manage it when it appears. Therefore, my thinking is that if we build these changes in the right ways, the usual pockets of dissatisfaction among teachers will be reduced, simply because they are incorporated as partners in the changes and we are supporting teachers as they wrestle with the complexities of making the changes work for themselves and for their students.

Also in this manuscript, I will *not* provide what most of the other change books have—here you will *not* see an endless set of "how to" lists for leaders to use as they attempt to orchestrate change. Instead, I will attempt to weave together a series of principles, concepts, and relationship-rich strategies to work toward sustaining the changes and ensuring the change's durability over time. There may be new knowledge for the reader for certain and, goodness knows, there may be even a few lists or checklists within the pages. Yet, the work here will be based on the idea that just as there is no quick, permanent fix to school problems, there is no quick and easy leadership book to guide the work so it will last. The emphasis here will be on that system of strategies, relationships, and operations that must exist over time if the much-needed improvements will have any chance at all.

A focus on the system of strategies, relationships, and operations will move us *away* from thinking of the school as the target of improvement (the traditional thinking), and toward the idea that a school leader's work is to essentially organize and create conditions in which the adults and students within the walls can flourish. I am reminded of a trusted colleague of mine who put it more succinctly: "Schools don't change; the *individuals* within schools must hold onto and demonstrate changed practices" (Hall & Hord, 2001). Therefore, if schools are more and more successful, it is because the individuals within the school walls are working in conditions that support their development, build relationships, and hold each other accountable for improvement, day by day. The *individuals* in schools should be where we focus our efforts of change—examining the comfort and organizational citizenship that will develop if the leader's actions, strategy, and empathy are singularly reflected in his or her core.

A Peek Inside

The pages here will invite dialogue, opinions, and provide guidance—intentionally so. Leaders in all sorts of "states" of success and tenure will find the pages useful. In order to help leaders explore their efforts and consider adjustments, I will invite all to review what we have known about effective leadership for years, perhaps re-introducing the reader to highly regarded research on change, leadership, communication, listening, and problem solving. This book is unique, though, in that it combines all of that research into a practical whole for the practitioner—weaving together the *why*, *what*, and *how* of school change. By aligning a series of interconnected concepts, each reader may create his or her own relationship-rich,

> Long-term leadership will reduce resistance and manage it when it appears.

> A school leader's work is to essentially organize and create conditions in which the adults and students within the walls can flourish.

personalized path for leading and managing change. Our work together will follow this path of concepts and ideas.

We will

- Examine the big picture of how change happens in organizations and how to observe change in terms of design-worthy, interconnected phases.

- Look at the leader's approach to change and how his or her personal preference for leading change may or may not influence or positively impact the efforts.

- Consider how the leader's approach to change may actually exacerbate the resistance to the change early on.

- Realize that the *what* and *why* of change must inform the *how*.

- Appreciate the specific strategies, operations, and relationships that enable the leader to initiate the change more successfully and reduce resistance to the change.

- See what begins to happen when people are attempting the changes at first and consider the issues they may have that may lead to an early abandonment of the change.

- Reflect on the kind of professional learning that the adults desire during the early attempts to try the changes, and understand why professional learning does not always meet those needs.

- Weigh the types of observed toxicity with teams and individuals as they begin to try the changes and consider what to do about it.

- Review the concept of rewards for the "early doers" and why this practice is so vital to sustaining momentum.

- Appreciate the time that is necessary for people to practice the changes in a sophisticated, student-oriented way.

- Examine the unique professional learning needs that people have when trying to implement the change successfully.

- Dig deep into the idea of enduring change, permanence, or institutionalization of the changes, when it happens and under what conditions, and how to recognize you are getting there.

- See simple intervention strategies and protocols when the resistance to the change seems to be chronic or overpowering.

- Study how to anticipate and remove barriers to the changes when moving toward institutionalization or permanence.
- Review a variety of resistance-reducing strategies and dialogue strategies to fill the leader's toolkit.

As said before, there is an implied and understood sequence to how enduring, effective change typically happens, but in each case the change you are leading may manifest itself in a different way. Additionally, during the journey of enduring change, it appears that there is no guaranteed way to predict the kind of resistance during each phase of change (if any) that may appear as we are moving toward permanence. The only guarantee is that resistance *may* happen at some point, and the leader's job is to first determine why the resistance is fundamentally understandable and whether or not to respond to it. Again, there are no recipes for handling the resistance—the only standard we must follow is to recognize that in many cases, the resistance is occurring for a good reason and, if appropriate, address it to validate while refocusing the individual's efforts. Illustrations of the uniqueness of each change and the kind of resistance that was addressed will be woven throughout the book to highlight real examples of the challenges two vastly different school districts faced as they initiated changes, focused on resolving problems while in the middle of a massive change, and attempted to build trust as they pushed hard for improvements.

As you might suspect, I'm a fan of face-to-face dialogue and work; for me, the visual and the verbal often combine to create a more accurate picture of the nuances of personal change my colleagues are facing. In our unsettled world, we will probably have to lead schools in creative and safe ways that still seek the kinds of relationships that combine with an unerring focus to achieve lasting results. Therefore, while many of my examples and strategies are based on traditional forms of communication, the savvy leader will immediately see ways the suggestions can be modified to build for lasting success in his or her school context.

I'm ready for a leadership reset. It is time to get out of the ever-spinning blender of short, limited results. It is time to invest in a lasting vision of a preferred future and realize that we can have it all—effective schools that are steadily moving toward better outcomes for students, teachers and students who find joy within the walls they inhabit, and leaders who find their focus and results in the concept of noticing and responding to issues instead of reacting to them. Read on, and let's work on this together.

CHAPTER 1

BUILD IT FOR THE LONG HAUL

Design, communicate, build, and lead the work with a deep understanding of and commitment to how change happens over time.

KEY PRACTICE

Nourish Change for a Long Life

Think about any significant school change you have been a part of. Essentially, the change was "triggered" by some decision that improvement was needed. Communication followed to the folks who would be directly involved in the change, and then the change was kicked off. They learned as much as they could about it, and after a certain period of time—when it was felt people were ready—the leaders began expecting the change to begin being practiced. Sometimes, as people were getting comfortable with the mechanics of the change, problems began to pop up. People may have become disenchanted with the change and even lobbied for the removal of it. If responses to the troubles were timely, transparent, and focused, with luck the change became a part of the practice and things eventually improved both for teachers and for students.

This description is an example of a large-scale attempted change in our schools. It would take a considerable amount of time for our change example to succeed. This example was a happy story, ending in success and permanence. It highlights a leader and teachers who rolled up their sleeves and invested in the work for the long haul. We want all of our school changes to take root and have long and prosperous lives. It may seem odd to think of any important change as having a "lifespan," but essentially that is what we have learned from change leaders over the past 40 years. Huberman and Miles (1984) and Fullan (2007) have documented that change develops in evolving cycles over time. Schools and districts are often involved in multiple initiatives at once—and the fact is that every big change project at school is different and carries its own set of contexts and variables. Because of these differences, leaders cannot lead each initiative in the same way. In addition, the relative "age" of the innovation should influence what the leader notices and how she or he supports the change with the people around her or him. The encouragers and motivators for people will differ and evolve over the life of the change (Fullan, 2007; Huberman & Miles, 1984).

In our previous successful example, there was a period of learning about the change, there was time spent on implementing the mechanics of the change, and there was a period when the work was about deepening the change in consistency and quality so it would become permanent and have lasting positive impact. This became the life span of the change, and the life span has an infancy period, a maturing period, and an older, wiser period of reflection and stability. If the school leader is to build change to last, he or she must not

Figure 1.1   The Life Span of School Change

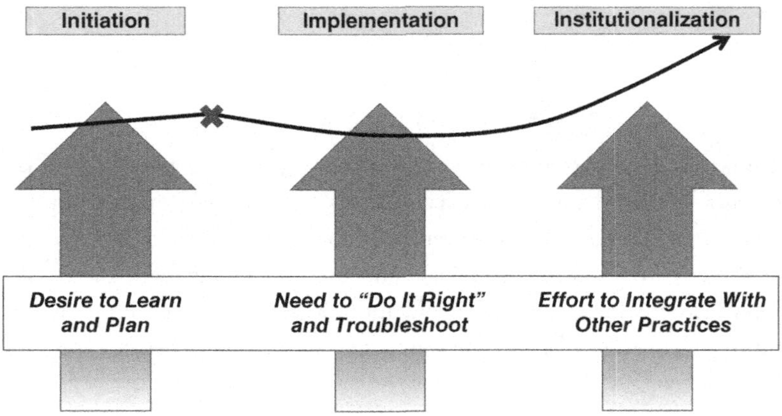

only know about the life span of change but also how to lead and manage it according to the age of the change at that moment. The infancy, maturing period, and the older stage of stability can be illustrated in three interconnected phases. Using Fullan's (2007) description of these life span phases, consider Figure 1.1, which graphically represents these change phases.

Figure 1.1 is a simple representation of the life of any change at the district or school level. We all keep our fingers crossed that the innovations we are leading become part of the fabric of the schools as they mature, grow, and become more impactful over time. The curved bold arrow in Figure 1.1 represents the years of development and evolution of the change. For instance, the graphic could illustrate a large-scale change from the beginning (the start of our bold arrow moving from left to right) to a point when the change was embedded into practice in a meaningful way (the point of the arrow). The whole illustrated process will more than likely take a number of years to become institutionalized. During those years of work, the needs and concerns of people doing the work will transform from (a) wanting to learn about the change to (b) trying out the change and troubleshooting in order to do it well, to (c) an attempt to integrate the change with other changes in the person's repertoire.

In Figure 1.1, you will also notice an "x" on the bold line, somewhere between initiation and beginning implementation. This identifies the beginning of the "implementation dip" (Fullan, 2001) and it's when people start having trouble making the change work. More detail about the implementation dip is found in the implementation section of this chapter.

It isn't earth-shattering to know that change has a life span and that people often experience issues when they try to make the change work. Just because we know these facts doesn't mean we lead according to it. Most of the changes we champion have very short lives in schools. Most of them never grow to maturity—the changes are abandoned long before they can really take hold—usually because the changes may be hard and cause some concerns and issues as they struggle to hold on to their lives.

This kind of short-term, failed change leadership must stop. Leaders must in fact lead, on a daily basis, with knowledge of the cycles of change and the determination to manage the changes according to the relative maturity of the change. This view of "change-related leadership" is both respectful to the people doing the work as well as more efficient and fluid, because the leader is pivoting according to the factors influencing the change.

Lead With a Deep Knowledge of Each Phase of Long-Term Change

If we are to lead on a daily basis with this change-related knowledge, we need detailed information and an operational understanding about the three phases. While these phases are often described and illustrated as three separate ones, it is important to remember that they overlap in practice. Each phase embraces not only leader actions but also participant actions, which combine to illustrate growth of the innovation and continuing evolution of practice.

Initiation Is Where We Establish the Why and What. Every long-term, important change has a birth or beginning. The impetus for the innovation can occur from the central office, the single decision from a school leader. It may occur after a long period of study, data analysis, and contemplation by one or multiple parties. Even though the beginning of a long-term improvement can feel exciting and hopeful, we must pay attention to this phase and allow it to develop fully.

When it becomes clear that "change is in the wind," people will want to have unrestrained access to information about the change so they can get a sense of a general, predictable understanding of the change with which they will be connected. Frequent and consistent communication between the leaders and his or her coworkers is critical during this early stage (Fullan, 2007). Other factors of equal importance relate to the scope of the change, pertinent time lines, and initial expectations for all involved. Attention to all of these variables, combined with a sense of clarity and transparency, tend to give people comfort—even if they know the innovation will require major adjustments in the way they work, they will probably be comforted by the wealth of knowledge and structure around the innovation.

Many of the questions from people will focus on "Why are we doing this?" and "What is this change, exactly?" Having a vision for the innovation—in other words, some clarity about what is being attempted to achieve and why we are doing it—is critical to people early on. I have learned, however, that if the vision for the change is developed or established too early in the life span of the change, there may not be enough understanding of the innovation to create clarity and comfort about the anticipated improvement. In other words, if the vision is struck too early in the process, it may actually alarm people and overwhelm them instead of providing the assurance and focus that people need. John P. Kotter (2012) warns against the vision being so lengthy or complicated that it loses its ability to energize and compel the work, leading instead to confusion or alienation. The big, elaborate, dense vision "neither rallied [people] together nor inspired change. In fact, they may have had just the opposite effect" (Kotter, 2012, p. 8). I am in favor of a compromise between the dense, lengthy, overwhelming vision that Kotter warns about and the kind of vision that is so short and vague that it could fit on a bumper sticker and gives no clear picture of what the organization is going to try to achieve. In other words, having a vision that is lengthy enough to really paint a "word picture" of what is trying to be achieved seems to be the guidance that people need. Any more than that, however, may overwhelm, madden, and actually fracture the culture. The vision should walk the fine line, then, between long and overwhelming and a catchy phrase. One should be able to read the vision and have a really clear sense of *what* this school is trying to achieve—what the future will look like.

Even though there may be widespread excitement and anticipation about the change, resistance can, in fact, appear very early in this very beginning. You might think that initiation is too early for people to formulate an opinion and develop negative communication and actions around it. Let's not be naïve. It can happen, even at the very beginning of the work. The January 1969 issue of the *Harvard Business Review*'s article titled "How to Deal with Resistance to Change" (Lawrence, 1969) detailed the kind of resistance that might appear at, what seems to the leader, illogical times. During initiation, people may already make the decision (with little understanding of the innovation) that they are incapable of making the kinds of measurable modifications in their practices that the innovation appears to demand (Lawrence, 1969). Lawrence named this a technical fear. A technical fear is real and valid to the person who is afraid of what will be demanded of him or her. Good leaders anticipate these fears and understand them so they will not be alarmed when they hear them being expressed. Chapter 2 will take a deep dive into initiation, how to lead and manage it, and what to do about issues that pop up during this early stage.

Implementation Is Where the Rubber Meets the Road. We say we have moved into implementation when we feel that we have learned enough about the innovation and have the structures in place to support individuals as they begin using the practices, materials, or program. Remember that during initiation, there is an emphasis on gaining knowledge about the innovation. This beginning knowledge, while critical, may be a bit shallow, because any training cannot replicate how the innovation will be in each person's classroom. Therefore, during early implementation, people will be trying to use the innovation based on what they learned during beginning training. In other words, they will attempt to use their own understanding of the innovation in a way that "seems right" to them (Tomlinson & Murphy, 2015).

During this early trial and error, individual experimentation is a good thing—it is the desirable behavior from people implementing their own versions of the change. As a college professor once told me, "Teachers do not adopt a new change; instead, they try to adapt the change to their practices" (G. Ponder, personal communication, fall 1993). During the early part of implementation, leaders have to continue to help people understand what changed, and what deep, sophisticated practice looks like so they can continue to compare it to their personal adaptation of the change. One of the dangers during implementation is that people will just rely on their own adapted interpretation of the innovation without the ability to compare their version with the intended version. If leaders neglect to model the intended sophistication and depth of the practice, individual teachers may grow content with their version of the change and begin to believe that unsophisticated practice is the innovation.

Even if the purpose of the innovation has been firmly established during initiation, it may begin to be lost in the day-to-day maze of demands on teachers. To prevent this, effective leaders will continue to stress the purpose of the change. This communication will help motivate participants so they can deepen the practices and begin to get results from their students. Deepening the practices to get results involves this internal cycle of individual trial, error, and adjustments in small ways. We must notice small attempts at integrating (adapting) the new practices into the person's repertoire of how he or she accomplishes work. When people make small changes and see results in their classroom contexts, they are more likely to continue the work and make additional efforts, because they have seen the payoff and have experienced little damage from these small actions. What people begin to believe about their ability to implement the innovation actually makes a difference in their personal motivation and personal achievement. The extent to which teachers develop competence with and confidence in their changing practices and see benefits to their students will alter the adults' behavior in positive ways (Tschannen-Moran, 2004).

> What people begin to believe about their ability to implement the innovation actually makes a difference in their personal motivation and personal achievement.

I don't know about you, but even the most effective implementation will not go perfectly. Resistance *will* almost assuredly appear during the implementation phase. To be honest, a certain amount of resistance during this phase actually makes sense. At first, during initiation, there is excitement about the innovation (even if it's dreaded, there is a certain energy about the possibilities of the change). People have had training on what the innovation is, and they know why it is needed.

They are attempting to think through how they will incorporate it in their classroom practices. As they make their initial efforts, they will encounter unanticipated hurdles or issues. Those issues could include (a) an awareness that their materials to support the innovation are inadequate; (b) they are experiencing classroom management difficulties because of new processes, arrangements, or procedures; or (c) they cannot seem to "get it all done" now within their time constraints because of the addition of the new practice. (Obviously, there is a myriad of other reasons people may experience difficulty during beginning implementation.) The range of troubles may aggregate into a general unhappiness about the innovation and a vocalized reluctance to continue the new practices. Commonly called the "implementation dip" (Fullan, 2007), this loss of enthusiasm actually signals both good and bad news to the leader. Look back in this chapter at Figure 1.1 to see a graphic illustration of the implementation dip (note the "x"). The good news about experiencing this lag in enthusiasm and performance is that people are generally trying the innovation out in their own classroom contexts. The bad news is that they are having a bit of trouble with it. This may be hard for you to buy, but from my own experiences, I can tell you that I had always preferred that my teachers were trying the innovation and having trouble with it than not attempting to try it at all!

As teachers are trying out the innovation, the leader is met with yet another challenge. If the beginning implementation issues leading to this enthusiasm "dip" are not addressed and adequately resolved for people, they may indeed abandon the innovation and go back to their former practices—and be quite satisfied with maintaining the status quo—which is what the schools are trying to alter. We will again take a deeper dive into implementation, see how resistance may look at this time in the change, and consider specific actions to lead implementation in chapter 3.

The "implementation dip" actually signals both good and bad news to the leader.

Institutionalization Is When the Change Becomes Part of Our Daily Wardrobe. I like to call institutionalization the phase of the work when people aren't calling "it" anything specific anymore. In other words, during implementation, when people are trying to get sophisticated practices under their belts, they still say "we are doing differentiation" or "we are implementing a new reading program" or "we are working to embed writing into all of our standard subjects." When nearing institutionalization, it seems that people don't often refer to it by name, because they have been working with the innovation so long and incorporating it into their own practices that the innovation has become a part of the fabric of the way the schools work. Another way to look at institutionalization is that people have turned the innovative improvements into refined routines, so ingrained into the fabric of the schools that they would outlast the presence of the leader (Sergiovanni, 1992).

The change that you have been championing, then, will either become embedded into practice or be discarded because of uneven or faulty implementation efforts. Often, we become impatient to "move on" to another big innovation and simply assume that because they have been working on the current innovation for some time, surely it will take hold. This is not the case. Even if implementation has gone well, issues have been worked out, and there is the culture and the structure to institutionalize the practice, there is still work to do. Competing innovations or issues must be directly addressed. Results have to be assessed. Teachers will continue to be reminded of the purpose of the innovation, supported for their continued efforts, and given opportunities for teachers to work together to make the practices even better.

You might think that if you have gotten this far and are stabilizing the innovation into regular practice, issues of resistance are just distant memories. Resistance may, though, appear during this mature phase of the innovation and surprise even the savviest leaders. Even if you have worked on implementation for years and feel really strongly that it has gone well, if people are met with other competing demands and cannot seem to figure out how to resolve the competition, they may vocalize frustration and abandon the innovation in favor of the new one. Even at this phase of change, the layering of innovations can seem to people like that constant change blender referred to in our introductory chapter. Thus, the leader must do what he or she can to affirm the vision, remind people of the benefits they are seeing, and remove obstacles or roadblocks to continued, better practice. In addition, the leader must ensure that the evolving culture of the school is supportive of these new, heightened practices. While John Kotter addresses institutionalization and culture in the business world, his words are relevant to us. "When the new practices made in a transformation effort are not compatible with the relevant cultures, they will always be subject to regression. Changes in a work group, a division, or an entire company can come undone, even after years of efforts, because the new approaches haven't been anchored firmly in group norms and values" (Kotter, 2012, p. 157). Figure 1.2 illustrates these phases in another way (Fullan, 2007; Kotter, 2012; Tomlinson & Murphy, 2015).

Figure 1.2   Phases of Change Implications for Leaders

CHANGE PHASE	NECESSARY ELEMENTS	GENERAL CONSIDERATIONS
Initiation	• Systematic examination of information signaling the need for a change • Clear establishment of a clear urgency for the change • Development of a vision to guide the change (late during Initiation) • Training to elevate knowledge level of the change • Adequate resources to get started	• Sources of information might include student performance information, informal conversations, or district directive. • A vision will tie the work to the urgency, and yet a vision established at the very beginning of the work may not be well-developed enough until people have a better sense of what the work will mean. • Professional learning in the form of training is often advised to guarantee a certain level of knowledge among the change participants.
Implementation	• Clear responsibilities for orchestration and troubleshooting • A focus on short-term "wins" to reward effort • Champions for the change at the school level • Job-embedded professional learning to support individual and collective efforts • Resource adjustment to acknowledge an awareness of how the change is progressing • Vision adjustment to continue focus • Plans to measure progress and remove obstacles	• While the district may initiate the change, in reality it cannot implement the change. Implementation is the school's responsibility and ownership must be transferred and felt. • There must be a mix of pressure (heat) and support (light). • Early implementers and champions should be rewarded in some way (more resources, extra time to plan, load reduction, more flexibility, etc.). • Leaders must be seen as understanding the change and capable of leading informal conversations with teachers about the progress they are making (non-evaluative). • Early on, measures of progress may not include student performance data but instead, teacher data, attitudes, efforts to implement, and what teachers are learning.
Institutionalization	• Integration of change into the school's usual practice • Elimination of competing practices • Links to other change efforts to communicate the unity of purposes • Widespread and refined use of the change • A school-based network of local practitioners and experts for continued access • Measurements of success using a variety of teacher and student indicators	• An indication of whether or not the change has been integrated may be that people are not referring to the change as "something they have to do." • Professional learning continues to be important at this phase but at the school level. • There is a perceived adjustment of practices to absorb and accommodate the change. • When the change has been institutionalized, many of the observed efforts of practice are at a sophisticated, refined level, yielding consistent results with students.

A deep knowledge of how to lead according to the age of the change is vital to leaders; just as important is a belief that the relationships that we cultivate will help propel the work into more lasting impact.

Lead With a "People-Sensitive Mindset" of How the Change Efforts Will Play Out

As we lead over the long haul, we invariably see areas for growth and change. Most often, the catalyst for change is to address an achievement gap or some kind of deficiency in the school. We feel the pressure to change things quickly, and in an attempt to find the solution, we frequently seek some program or quick solution to "apply" to the problem. We feel that if we just find the right "fix" to our issue, things can change quickly and for the better. The danger with this kind of thinking is that it may encourage us to drift toward the more "scientific" or "technical" approach to leading. This view of leading focuses on the incremental analysis of specific issues—the result of which is often the loss of the big picture in what makes an organization like a school work. The scientific/technical approach relies on the positioning of programs, mandates, and resources without paying much attention to the realization that no particular program, mandate, or resource will work long term unless the people implementing such remedies are not only committed to the work but have continued to acquire the skills necessary for implementation success. In other words, we search for the solution but forget that the people with whom we work will be the ones implementing it!

Over the years, I have come to the hard realization that we often unintentionally ignore the very people who are expected to do real, hard work. They deserve better. They deserve empathy, time, consideration, and freedom to take risks and make adjustments. I strongly believe that leaders can (and must) really have it all—strategic, operational actions to improve things *and* deep, meaningful, collaborative relationships with the people doing the work. But there is a caution. "Working *with* teachers instead of *on* them involves a series of flexible [leader] efforts to develop and support their intrinsic motivation for personal learning and development" (Tomlinson & Murphy, 2015, p. 39). So, working with teachers while maintaining a focus and the pressure for action becomes the formula for sustaining the innovation until it has an impact on not only those teachers but also students in their care. Leaders do not have to choose to be a hard-driving technical leader or a soft, relationship-rich leader. It is not one or the other. It is both. See Figure 1.3.

Figure 1.3   The Leader's Simultaneous Approach

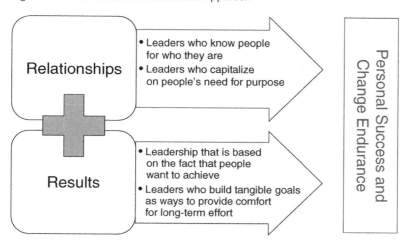

The work of effective leaders is a constant balance of pressure and support, or "heat" and "light." It is obvious that people will respond in different ways to this combination of heat and light. Their responses will manifest behaviors differently over the life span of the innovation (Fullan, 2007; Huberman & Miles, 1984). In addition, individuals will respond to the innovation both emotionally and behaviorally as they begin to understand the change, get deeper into it, feel personal struggles, and work to ensure its lasting continuation (Hall & Hord, 2001). Therefore, we can't lead with both relationships and results in mind unless we know what these two concepts look like at each phase of long-term change.

Leaders can (and must) really have it all—strategic, operational actions to improve things *and* deep, meaningful, collaborative relationships with the people doing the work.

Take a Moment

This chapter has highlighted the long-term phases of change, critical to leaders' knowledge and actions. The science and practice of leading initiation, implementation, and institutionalization have been with us for many years. The question that must be asked is this: why, then, do so many efforts fail? The problem seems to be that many leaders, in spite of their understanding of how changes happen over time, do not *act* on or use what they know. To put it another way, "a commitment to these ideas is only a partial victory" (Tomlinson & Murphy, 2015). If leaders continue to lead in opposition to what we know about long-term change, they stand the chance of seeing and feeling substantial resistance to valid efforts to improve. Therefore, the first critical skill for leaders is to commit to the concepts undergirding long-term change and lead, on a daily basis, according to that understanding.

(Continued)

(Continued)

We will delve into each of these phases of the life of your change in the subsequent chapters. Five key leadership actions—establishing the purpose, listening to concerns, establishing trust, designing powerful professional learning, ensuring short-term successes—will be embedded in each chapter devoted to the particular phase. These five concepts weave together a blueprint for each of us that I call an "architecture." The architecture is useful when we are orchestrating the necessary improvements in our schools and is represented in Figure 1.4.

Figure 1.4   Change Architecture

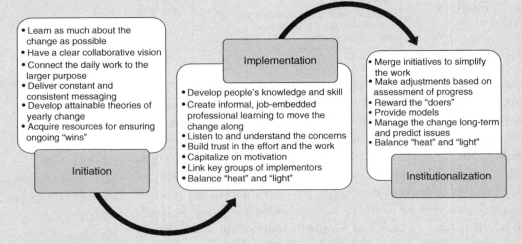

Source: Bossidy & Charan, 2009; Farina & Kotch, 2014; Fullan, 2007; Hirsh, Psencik, & Brown, 2014; Huberman & Miles, 1984; Tomlinson & Murphy, 2015

We will not only explore resistance in each phase of change but also in a separate chapter, along with separate chapters on critical topics in our architecture shown in Figure 1.4.

At this point, let's learn about two dramatically different school districts— Kingsport City Schools in Kingsport, a small city in the far northeast part of Tennessee, and the Ashton Unified School District, a large urban school district in the northwest part of the country. We will see the ways leaders in those districts not only prepared for big changes in their schools but also how they approached looming problems and attempted to resolve them or eliminate them before they were met with consistent resistance. The leaders in these districts were not perfect, but they were devoted to leading and managing the change in a relationship-rich, sequential, and understandable way. In some ways, both sets of district leaders were highly successful; and in other ways, they were not. All of the leaders from the two districts gave me permission to use their actual district names and their individual names. The Kingsport City Schools district, therefore, really exists as do the three leaders who will describe the change they sought, and no names have been changed for this publication. At the time of publication, however, it was decided to anonymize the names of the district now referred to as "Ashton Unified School District" and the four Ashton Unified leaders who were interviewed. This district did not enjoy the luxury of seeing their efforts work smoothly toward institutionalization. The disguising of names was done out of respect for the hardworking district leaders so there was a degree of protection from any negative reactions anyone might have from reading about their struggles. What you should understand, however, is that these two case studies were very real; and you will read about their long-term change efforts in unvarnished, transparent documentation of actions, successes, and dismays. We will look at their highs and their lows, and their experiences will give us opportunities to reflect on why both may have happened. We will certainly benefit from these insights.

A SNAPSHOT OF OUR TWO SCHOOL DISTRICTS ATTEMPTING CHANGE

The leaders of our two districts, Kingsport City Schools, in northeast Tennessee, and the Ashton Unified School District, in the northwest part of the country, were eager to implement important changes. As we study these two example districts, we will learn (a) their context and (b) the change they sought. At the end of each chapter on initiation, implementation, and institutionalization, you will see how the leaders of each district planned for and handled that phase.

Kingsport City Schools	Ashton Unified School District
Location: Kingsport, Tennessee	Location: Northwest United States
Enrollment: 7,426	Enrollment: 48,500
81% White; 11% African American; 5% Hispanic; 2% Asian or Pacific Islander; 1% Native American	41% White; 16.9% Asian or Pacific Islander; 15.7% Biracial or multiracial; 11.6% Hispanic; 8.8% Native American; 4.9% African American
38% Economically Disadvantaged	43% Economically Disadvantaged
11 Schools	63 Elementary Schools

As you can see, Kingsport City Schools and the Ashton Unified School District are dramatically different from each other in multiple ways. The leaders of each district attempted a major change in their schools and tried to design their actions to align with what they knew about long-term change. The actions described throughout the next few chapters will illustrate what worked for them and what didn't work as each set of leaders sought to deepen instructional practices with their teachers and achieve greater achievement with all of their students. The following detail will help you understand a little more about each district and the goal of the changes for each.

Kingsport City Schools

Kingsport City Schools is a small rural district in the northeast corner of Tennessee. While it enjoys a long reputation for academic excellence, there is a consistently noticeable gap in achievement between White students and students of other demographic categories. The 11 school principals historically have been champions of independent thinking and resist the push to standardize their practices across all 11 schools. Fiercely independent, those principals *do* work together on a regular basis and accomplish much; however, they strongly believe that each of their schools is unique and deserves leadership that builds from the unique culture there.

At least 10 years ago, the district employed instructional coaches in the district to work with all schools and all levels and subject areas. These were teachers on special contracts who primarily worked with teachers to improve instruction. At that time, the decision of "which teachers should I work with?" was made by district officials. The charge to the instructional coaches was to focus almost solely on the teachers in buildings who were *least* instructionally successful.

This method of assigning instructional coaches to the neediest teachers continued for several years. Over time, however, district officials and principals began to realize that these targeted teachers were not making improvements as quickly as desired; they also noticed a prevailing sense among all of the other teachers in buildings to avoid instructional coaches because the assignment of a coach to a teacher meant that you were "in trouble." It became very apparent to district decision makers that the role of the instructional coach needed to be reviewed and changed.

In 2016, I was asked to contract with Kingsport and rethink the role of the instructional coach. The director at that time wanted a complete overhaul; in fact, he wanted to virtually erase the vision of the previous instructional coaching program and replace it with something more effective—and he wanted this from the "ground up." His vision was to then initiate the new coaching system and to work to effectively institutionalize the new coaching version for years to come.

The Ashton Unified School District

The Ashton Unified School District is a large, mostly urban district in the northwest part of the country. The district is organized into loose "areas," with directors supervising the principals in those areas and assisting principals in making decisions for area improvement. Teacher instruction and student achievement in the district has historically been uneven and spotty. Some schools enjoy focused principals and committed staff members who realize consistently high student achievement. Some schools, however, are described by district leaders as less focused. These schools do not achieve consistently effective achievement with their students.

The diversity of the school district is high and in marked contrast to the diversity in the Kingsport City Schools. Because of the diverse nature of students and their experiences and the inconsistent and variable achievement, a decision was made in 2015 to study and purchase a new reading program for the elementary grades K–5. The thinking, according to district leaders, was that there was a huge need to provide consistently effective instruction to all of the diverse students, raising the floor for achievement and creating a common teaching language among all 63 elementary schools in the "science of reading." Materials were purchased to launch the change, and plans were made to provide professional learning for people about the new program.

New materials were purchased for all of the participating grades, and the decision was made to only initiate and implement the materials in the K–2 classes during the first year. The district leaders' theory was to allow a "phase in" of the change. During the second year of work, leaders would continue their support of the K–2 teachers while initiating the change with the grades 3–5 teachers. So, prior to the K–2 first year of initiation, there was widespread voluntary training for those teachers participating in the change, led by consultants of the company providing the materials. The training appeared to be effective based on simple measures and, in fact, there was a certain energy and enthusiasm for the new materials as expressed by teachers.

Initiation and beginning implementation were not smooth across the district, and I was asked by the Ashton Unified School District to begin consulting with them in late 2018 as a result of a bargaining contract between the Ashton Unified School District and the local teacher union affiliated with the National Educational Association (NEA). The purpose of my ongoing facilitation contract between Ashton and the local NEA was to provide an "outside voice" and support in resolving the multiple implementation issues and the widespread dissatisfaction that stemmed from the reading program change.

In the next chapters, we will follow these two districts as they initiate and implement their desired changes.

CHAPTER 2

GIVING INITIATION THE ATTENTION IT DESERVES

Remind people of the *what, why,* and *how* of the change in order to build trust in the purpose and appreciate any early resistance.

KEY PRACTICE

Take the Time to Start the Right Way

Several times in my career and in various parts of the country, I have been involved with summer professional learning for principals and district leaders. I lose count when I remember all of the times that the superintendent took that opportunity to announce, "Here are our major initiatives for this year." As she details those major initiatives for *this year*, I watch her audience. Her remarks are almost always met with polite responses and even some visible excitement, but I can imagine that their conversations in their heads (some I can't print here!) include "What will this be?" or "What will it look like?" or "More changes?" or "Are you kidding me?" I'm not necessarily saying that the superintendent was wrong in wanting some changes; rather, I'm suggesting that she is sending a dangerous operational message. I am always afraid that her announcement of "this year's priorities" imply that these major initiatives will be easily launched, incorporated, and managed within a short time frame. This notion is simply wrong.

Successful change and deep improvement rarely happen within a year's worth of work. By her using the phrase "for this year," she is implying just that. The typical summer training announcements are supposed to magically begin the changes, and yet they reinforce my long-standing worry that we do not do ourselves any service when we simply announce a change and then somehow expect it to magically take off and work efficiently after one, two, or three days of training. Effective leaders know that starting the change takes time. Successful initiation moves people forward into the change from carefully choreographed plans and sensitive responses to a wide variety of issues. As effective leaders consider big changes in their schools, they will give initiation as much consideration as they do the actual work of implementation. This chapter will focus on the effective initiation of any change when the intent is institutionalized improvement, a powerful collaborative culture, and enhanced student and teacher performance.

You will remember that the initiation of the change is the "process that leads up to and includes a decision to adopt or proceed with the change" (Fullan, 2007, p. 69). From my experience, a successful start to a change may take several weeks to several months. The driving force behind the change may come from a variety of reasonable sources. It may come from the state or provincial agency, from the district office, as a single decision by a school leader, or it may occur after a collaborative period of study, data analysis, and contemplation.

Provide Timely Information and Be Sensitive to Feelings

Whatever the force behind the change, you can be assured that people will be talking about it even before they start the change. As soon as they hear about the change, much of their discussion may focus on the need to acquire as much information about the change as they can (Hall & Hord, 2001). They may also be interpreting their perceptions of the change within their own individual contexts. By that, I mean that they may be examining the change or their perception of the change in terms of how much or how little the change will affect them (Hall & Hord, 2001). Fullan (2007) reminds us that during the initiation of the change, it may not matter who or what initiated the change as much as how teachers feel about their perceived understanding of the change and how it will change their personal lives.

During the start of the change, then, the leader must build a variety of ways that the people affected by the change will learn more about it. A fundamental beginning understanding of the change will be vital if the leaders are needing people to begin to form a common language about the change and generally get on board. Often, training is the vehicle to deliver information about the change, and it is generally an effective design for valuable beginning understanding of the change. Our superintendent in this chapter felt that training was perfect to kick off the initiatives; and in part, she was right. Training is an effective and often efficient way to disseminate information about the change because it can be replicated for a variety of audiences and we can control the trainer, thus ensuring some degree of expertise in the presentation.

We also have to be aware of training's limitations. Good leaders provide training when the conditions are just right for people to be motivated to gain some new understanding of the coming change. Training during the summer is often the wrong time for this. Right before school, training is usually met with dread, not enthusiasm, because the timing of the training just isn't right. We all know that schools function within a predictable yearly cycle—and right before the summer. I can assure you that teachers are much more concerned about their classrooms, materials, lesson plans, and class lists than acquiring knowledge about a change that will perhaps put another burden on them. In addition to the timing issue, training sheds very little light on the kinds of implementation issues people may have when they get serious about putting the change into practice. In other words, training may be excellent for providing beginning information, but it is an ineffective design to help teachers figure out practical ways to use the innovation. So, the savvy leaders will usually incorporate training into the initiation phase as a way to help people learn about the change in a uniform way but move to other professional learning designs as people begin implementing the change. As we will see throughout the book, professional learning is also needed throughout the implementation of the change, and yet the design for professional learning will change based on how to most effectively help the teachers at that point in the life of the change.

People Will Make Assumptions About the Change

As people are getting more information about the change, they will begin to make assumptions about the implications of the change on them in a personal way (Hall & Hord, 2001). Questions like "How will this affect me?" and "How much time will this take me to plan to implement this?" and "Am I the only one who is really going to work on this—will others be able to avoid it?" will be common internally considered questions for adults at school. Even the most effective teachers will wonder about how they will be able to adapt this new change into their practice without completely disrupting their daily work rhythms. For some, the change may be viewed as a burden if leaders are not sensitive to this concern and do not find ways to relieve this internal pressure on the folks who are about to be held responsible for the implementation of the new practice.

Leaders often find themselves in a position where they are the recipients of the change, and they themselves are not fully aware of the purpose of the change. This will make it a steep climb to be able to communicate the purpose of the change to teachers at their buildings. And yet, if a change is handed to them, leaders still have to work to find the purpose of the change and be able to articulate that successfully to their teachers. I always say that if the leaders cannot describe the new work succinctly and clearly help people see the moral underpinnings of the work, they shouldn't be asking teachers to do the work. They simply have no business asking hardworking individuals to devote themselves to the difficult work when they, themselves, cannot describe the value of the change.

Appreciate Any Early Resistance

It may seem farfetched that there would be any resistance to the change before the idea has even operationally begun. Yet, sensitive school leaders will be tuned in to early issues and will anticipate the needs people have early on, allowing them to manage the resistance better and stay dedicated to the purpose of the change. During initiation, the needs people have will vary according to the school, the context of the culture, and other competing pressures. In general, these needs may manifest themselves in some degree of resistance if people believe their needs might not be met. Because of this, leaders must appreciate the resistance they hear, because it signals that people are thinking about the change and are trying to sort it out. It also tells leaders what people may be fearing.

Whatever the responses to the initiation of the change, leaders will want to be sensitive to the kinds of needs people have when considering the change. Three needs or "wants" will generally pop up at the beginning of the change:

- People doing the work will want as much information about the change as possible.
- People will want to know how the change will personally affect them.
- People will want to know the larger reason, or purpose, of the change.

It is not hard to see how the absence of any one of these three needs may result in early resistance to the idea of the change. A deeper exploration of each will provide insights as to how to address each and may help leaders anticipate resistance issues.

Provide as Much Information as Possible. If teachers do not get adequate knowledge about the change through professional learning (usually training), they may form early and possibly incorrect opinions about the change, which may deter implementation or lead to ineffective implementation of the change. For instance, a teacher or groups of teachers may not have all of the information they need to begin developing strategies for implementation; because of this, they may implement the change as they see it but with only part of the information they need to eventually do it well. An example will illustrate this.

My wife, a former reading specialist, had a revelation when she was working with a district from home. She had been providing professional learning on the components of a balanced approach to literacy. Months after that training, she visited a series of classrooms and discovered that, because of partial understanding of the balanced literacy components, some teachers had equated a "balanced approach to literacy" with "pulling guided reading groups each day." That idea is not in itself incorrect; and yet, when she saw these guided reading groups, she came to realize that all of the groups in each visited teacher's class were virtually doing the same work in the same way.

Clearly, the teachers were implementing the change as best as they could with the knowledge they had. While their actions were not intended to be overtly resistant, the lack of understanding could lead to eventual sustained resistance because the results of their superficial efforts to learn about it and implement it would not be self-affirming and would not lead to the kind of achievement they wanted. Insufficient understandings of any change might lead to an early disregarding of the entire change because "it doesn't work for me or my kids."

Help People Understand How the Change Will Personally Affect Them. Leaders will also notice that a teacher needs to know how this change will affect them. Hall and Hord (2001) describe this need as a "self" need or egocentric approach to the change. Their personal concerns, while they may not seem that urgent or consequential to the leader, are real for the change implementer. If people are having these kinds of concerns, they are "uncertain about the demands of the innovation, his or her inadequacy to meet those demands, and his or her role with the innovation. This includes analysis of his or her role in relation to the reward structure of the organization, decision-making, and consideration of potential conflicts with existing structures or personal commitment" (Hall & Hord, 2001, p. 63).

As the teacher wonders how this change may affect them, he attaches personal feelings to the change (Hall & Hord, 2001). As he learns more about the change and begins to understand the rationale for the change, inevitably, he may grow curious or even suspicious of his role in the change and how the change will alter his sense of current safety. Feelings about the anticipated change will emerge. In other words, the challenge of initiation is in the space that lies "above and below our necks" (Kegan & Lehey, 2009). Because a potential immunity to change "expresses the thinking and feeling dimensions of a given level of mental complexity," both intellectual and emotional dimensions must be addressed to achieve real, adaptive change and decrease the possibility of resistance (Kegan & Lehey, 2009, p. 214). In essence, then, the leader's duty is to make sure that during the initial phase of the change, a clarification of the change itself and rationale for it (thinking about it) is vital. Equally important is knowing how people are personally reacting or responding to the change (feeling about it) must be part of the leader's overall overt strategy.

Invite Them Into the Rationale, or Purpose, of the Change. As people are learning about the change and wondering how it will personally affect them, they will naturally and inevitably want to know the *why* for the change. The why, or purpose, is uniquely important at the beginning of the work, and we will see that it is equally important as the work is progressing. At first, people will want to know how this new change is connected to the other work they are doing. In the absence of a clear purpose, there is a danger that people will look at the change as "another thing we have to do," not seeing the connection between the change and other mandates as well as feeling that there is a general "piling on" of initiatives that they are supposed to address—and address well. As I have said earlier, our responsibility as leaders is to (a) know how the change is connected to the other work and (b) know the larger reason, or the purpose, of the change. The larger reason, or purpose, of the change is *not* to raise student achievement test scores. While that may be an outcome of the focused change, it will not be a compelling reason for the change at the schools.

The compelling reason for the change is bigger than raising test scores. The reason or purpose speaks to the idea of what the people inside the school's walls are trying to achieve. Simon Sinek (2009) explains the importance of the purpose as knowing the *why*: "Knowing your why is not the only way to be successful, but it is the only way to maintain a lasting success and have a greater blend of innovation and flexibility. When a why grows fuzzy, it becomes much more difficult to maintain the growth, loyalty, and inspiration that helped drive the original success. By difficult, I mean that manipulation rather than inspiration fast becomes the strategy of choice to motivate behavior. This is effective in the short-term but comes at a high cost in the long term" (p. 50).

"Why are we doing this?" is a challenging and legitimate question for leaders. As we start the changes, we must know that people want to make sense of the change and will be motivated by that sense of the *why*. Pink (2009) puts it like this: "The most deeply motivated people—not to mention those who are most productive and satisfied—[want to] hitch their desires to a cause larger than themselves" (p. 131). The *why*, then, is the purpose for the work; and during the early phase of the work, it is one of the devices that teachers use to not only make sense of the change but also understand the "moral" ramifications of the work. If addressing the feelings people may have about starting the change is important, equally important is the need teachers will have about the *why* of the change. As we have said before, in the absence of a clear purpose, there is a danger that people will look at the change as "another thing we have to do," not seeing the connection between the new change and the other mandates.

Sometimes as leaders, we think that teachers should just understand that we wouldn't ask them to do something unless it was important. Or, we feel that people just need to get on with their business and "do the right thing and accept the change because *we* told them to do it."

I can't tell you how many school leaders have told me in trainings that "all this talk about purpose is worthless. We just need to document teachers if they will not get on board." This idea of simply putting more pressure on teachers to "get on board" usually has the opposite of the effect we want (Zuckoff & Gorscak, 2015). Folks will sometimes just wait out changes when they feel pressured and are not given the chance to embrace the purpose. Resistance to the change, then, will claim early footing before much of an effort has happened to implement it.

Leadership Essential Actions During Initiation

One of our case study districts enjoyed a relatively smooth initiation of their change, while the other appeared to have made some missteps in assuming that smooth implementation would naturally follow a brief initiation. Remember that initiation is a change phase dedicated to the *preparation* of people to be successful with the change. It is "the process that leads up to and includes a decision to adopt or proceed with the [implementation] of the change" (Fullan, 2007, p. 69). That anticipatory process requires planning, actions, and attention to people if it is to go smoothly. Those planning and responding actions are embedded in our "change architecture," explained in chapter 1. Embedded in that architecture as unifying threads are five essential actions that should be in the leaders' repertoire when the change is initiated. While these five essential actions pertain to initiation in this chapter, the same five actions will also be vital during implementation and institutionalization. For each phase in the life of the change, the five actions will vary in goal, scope, and action. For now, we will explore these five essential actions within the context of initiation and the reduction of early, organized resistance to the change. Remember that the goal of initiation is to provide a smooth pathway from "learning about the change" to "beginning to do it." After our review of these essential initiation actions, we will see how both of our districts applied them to their particular contexts.

Action #1: Collaboratively Construct the Purpose/ Vision and Strategically Message It

Daniel Pink (2009) identifies purpose as one of the three most important motivators for people. During initiation of a major school improvement change, people will question the rationale for it. That simple question is an attempt by a teacher or teachers to "put it all together" in their minds and see the importance of this particular change at this particular time. Schools function like both complex educational and social organizations; gone are the days when leaders could just command a change and people would fall in line simply because of the leader's charisma or authority. In today's world, the authoritarian or command style of leading will probably lead to being ignored or pretending to cooperate while quietly undermining the effort (Kotter, 2012). We have seen that this pressure to change may communicate a negative message: "There is something wrong with you. You're no good the way you are" (Zuckoff & Gorscak, 2015, p. 37). Therefore, having a cause that is grounded in an overall, passionate purpose during early initiation is essential not only to galvanize people but also to reduce the opportunities for resistance.

In most cases, the purpose of the work is articulated in the vision for their school. The vision for the school should describe "what we intend to become" when the major change initiatives have been successful. Leaders are often charged with completing or revising the vision for their schools. They, however, must avoid the trap of feeling the pressure for a clear vision and developing it themselves without the varied voices of the teachers who work within the school's walls. The development of the school's vision, involving as many people as possible, will be the most important action in identifying the purpose.

You can imagine, then, that the vision for the school drives the work. The vision also becomes both a filter and an aligning tool for the school. If held tightly, the vision will be examined in terms of a new initiative or change; if the new change "fits" with the vision, it might be initiated. If the new change doesn't seem to fit or people cannot see how the new change aligns with the major work already in place, perhaps the new initiative should not be considered.

The vision is an important part of the initiation of major work. That would mean that at the beginning of the important work, in the absence of the school vision, a leader must collaboratively describe the purpose through a thoughtful vision of what the school intends to become. Reeves and Eaker (2019) strongly support the act of creating a shared vision, saying that "during the first one hundred days, leaders must also build a strong foundation of shared values and collective commitments" (p. 77). If you believe that the vision is essential in the initiation of any major change—but a vision for the school already exists and has for several years—then the work during initiation would be to show how the new change would support the existing shared values already established. The leader's job, in this case, is to show how the new change will *accelerate and enhance* the quality of the vision as well as show how the new work aligns with the work people are already doing.

While I do not agree that the casting or recasting of a vision must be in the first 100 days of the leader's tenure at that school (Reeves & Eaker, 2019), I do believe that one of the leader's roles is to determine the alignment of the new suggested change with the other initiatives in place, collaboratively develop a new vision that describes our purpose in our future statement, and communicate clearly and often the vision on a daily basis. This constant reminding of the alignment of the work and how the new change will enhance the work is not only useful but also urgent as people are learning about the change and wondering whether or not this new change will matter.

Constructing and Messaging the Purpose During Initiation

Why Is This Action Important?	What If It Doesn't Happen?
Establishes the change as a high priority	People may re-prioritize the change in the absence of clarity from the principal.
Develops a way to help people "picture" the change in action	People may bring their own connotations to the change and misjudge the intent of the change.
Keeps reminding teachers the *why* for the change as they begin preparing to implement the change	If the vision and purpose are only stressed at the very beginning of the change, when people begin to think about implementing it, the vision/purpose may have become "fuzzy" due to lack of regular conversation.
Boosts energy and reminds people of the *why*	People may become less motivated and less unified in what they are intending to achieve.

Action #2: Listen and Be Empathetic to Early Concerns

During initiation, it is important to offer an empathetic ear to the people who will be eventually doing the implementation work. The leader's goal is to demonstrate acceptance of the feelings people are having and encourage them to remember that they and their work are worthwhile (Zuckoff & Gorscak, 2015). Listening to teachers will provide the mechanism for encouragement and empathy as they sort out their feelings and need for information. Listening *about* the change is vastly different from listening to see how you can *persuade* people to embrace the change. When I think of convincing people to accept the change, I immediately imagine the act of pushing them toward it. This exertion of pressure may be perceived as just that—pressure—and could convey the false assumption that the leader's words are far more important than the teacher's. The tactic of force does not lead to long-term collaboration, trust, and commitment. Listening *about* the change sends a different message and is actually one of the leader's key skills during initiation. What we know is this: when the teacher feels accepted and heard, there is less need to focus her mental and emotional energy on protecting herself (Zuckoff & Goscak, 2015).

These initial teacher reflections may take the form of concerns or worries about this future alteration in their daily practice. Hall and Hord describe the central idea of concerns people have during any time in the change and the key role leaders can play in meeting these concerns head on. They describe the research that finds that the more successful schools are places where the leader is having "very small, almost unnoticed interventions called incidents" (Hall & Hord, 2001, p. 67). These interventions, however, look nothing like traditional interventions. In Hall and Hord's actions, leaders are choosing to have these short conversations with teachers in an attempt to hear the concerns those teachers may have and to demonstrate understanding without altering the school's purpose and vision.

In fact, the leader, especially during the early initiation, should not assume that he or she completely understands the teacher's point of view; instead, his role is to listen, ask questions, and lightly probe to get to the source of the concern that the teacher has with the change (Hall & Hord, 2001). While these concerns may lie along a wide range of worries, during the early part of the change many worries will, as we have already learned, center on the need for information about the change, the rationale for the change, and how it will personally affect them.

If these small, incidental conversations are considered to be interventions (Hall & Hord, 2001), then the question becomes "what do I do about it as the leader of this change?" It may surprise you to know that more often than not, just the act of listening provides the assurance, trust, and a platform for personal or information issues. That trusting platform may be enough to suspend long-lasting resistance to the change. I have used these short listening episodes on many occasions (usually lasting no more than three minutes!) and have found that sometimes, if I solve the concern for them, people will take my solution as another way I am demeaning their intelligence or action regarding the change. You may feel that would never happen to you; however, I must caution you against the act of jumping too quickly to a solution. Remember that during the early stages of initiation, people want to still be affirmed for who they are and their efforts long before the change began. One goal of effective initiation is to prepare people for an open embrace of the change. Listening may be the most powerful way to send the message that teachers are partners with us in the change process and that their feelings are valid and must be heard.

The tactic of force does not lead to long-term collaboration, trust, and commitment.

Listening to Early Concerns People Have

Why Is This Action Important?	What If It Doesn't Happen?
Helps form an empathetic partnership between you and teachers	People may feel that they can't talk about their worries with leaders.
Reinforces the efforts people are making to embrace the change	People may feel that their efforts are "not good enough" and harshly judge their own competence.
Gives leaders insights as to what the problems might be or what people need at this time	Leaders might make mistakes in assuming they understand how to support people.
Models the kind of behavior we are expecting to see schoolwide	Teachers may unfairly judge leaders as not demonstrating the kind of empathetic behavior they expect teachers to use in their classrooms.

Action #3: Provide Pathways for People to Acquire What They Need to Be Good at It

A pressing need early on during initiation of the change will be for information about the change—what is it, how does it look, what materials are necessary for the change, how much time will it take, what are the results of other schools that have implemented the change, and so forth. Traditionally, one of the first steps in providing information is to ask teachers to participate in professional learning specifically about the change. The purpose for professional learning is to allow people to grasp new ideas, ask their big questions about the change, and begin to think about how they will integrate the change into their existing practices (Farina & Kotch, 2014).

All teachers who are being asked to not only consider the change but accept and implement it will, hopefully, learn about the change and the research behind it along with pertinent information about the change. We know that this initial professional learning usually takes the form of training. Training remains as usually the most efficient and valuable form of professional learning if the outcomes include (a) information or knowledge about the change, (b) the theory or research behind it, (c) modeling or glimpses of how the change might look in the classroom, and (d) conversations about the skills needed to be successful in the change (Joyce & Showers, 2003). In the initiation phase, therefore, it might be that training is necessary to provide all four of these essential components. One would hope that the training not only supplies these outcomes but also instills an energy or enthusiasm for the purported change. Training that aligns the outcomes of the sessions with the purpose or vision of the change is destined to be much more successful than training where the participants have to work hard to see the connection.

It has been my experience that if the early initiation training does not adequately supply the four outcomes previously listed, teachers may begin to reflect negatively on the change and suggest that this new set of practices are "simply another thing to do" without relevance to the purpose of the school. The leader's fluidity in designing and providing different forms of professional learning, then, becomes one of her most important skills. I strongly believe that the way professional learning looks and the goals for it should change over the life span of the change. If we can look at professional learning as "a constant and deliberate focus throughout the life span of the initiative, then the design for adult learning will change over time in response to progress and individual needs (Tomlinson & Murphy, 2015, p. 66). In other words, I like to say that training may be your best friend during initiation in order to get the same message out to large numbers of implementing teachers. However, it will be the *last* design teachers want when they are in the midst of implementing the change. When we deeply explore implementation in the next chapter, we will see other professional learning designs that are more likely to be well suited to that stage of actually trying the change practices out in our classrooms.

> Training may be your best friend during initiation in order to get the same message out to large numbers of implementing teachers. However, it will be the *last* design teachers want when they are in the midst of implementing the change.

Creating Ways for People to Get Good at the Change

Why Is This Action Important?	What If It Doesn't Happen?
Creates a uniform enthusiasm and knowledge base for the change	People may interpret the meaning of the change in different ways.
Provides a variety of ways that people can process their learning about the change	People's individual differences in learning will not be respected.
Prepares teachers for implementation with the research, how it may look, and the skills needed to use it in the classroom	Teachers may feel ill-equipped to think about implementation.

Action #4: Build Their Trust in You, the Work, and Each Other

It probably goes without saying that a deep sense of trust is critical if people are going to initiate and sustain an important change at school. Megan Tschannen-Moran defines trust as "one's willingness to be vulnerable to another based on the confidence that the other is benevolent, honest, open, reliable, and competent" (Tschannen-Moran, 2004, p. 17). Trust is a big idea that tends to be hard to describe. Trust is dynamic in that it can change over the course of time or over the course of the relationship as interdependence among the people in the school community changes. Sinek (2009) concurs, commenting that "trust is a feeling, not a rational experience. We trust people and companies even when things go wrong, and we don't trust others even though everything might have gone exactly as it should have. A completed checklist does not guarantee trust. Trust begins to emerge when we have a sense that another person or organization is driven by things other than their own self gain" (p. 84).

Sinek (2009) helps us understand the relationship of trust to values. "You have to earn trust by communicating and demonstrating that you share the same values and beliefs. You have to talk about your *why* and prove it with *what* you do" (p. 85). Sinek effectively aligns the importance of trust with two critical needs people will have during the early initiation of the change. In essence, he is saying that as people get started on a major change, they will want to know if their *why* is connected to others in the organization. Similarly, people will want to see the first steps (clarity about the *what*) toward the *why* to be clear and directly associated with it.

If trust is more of a feeling or a perception of the alignment of the *why* and *what*, then what are leader actions to promote trust during the early stages of the change? Fullan (2007) suggests that one skill for leaders is to show empathy with teachers in the difficult or trying circumstances of early change while maintaining the message and keeping clear on the vision. The leader, during initiation, alternately applies pressure (maintaining the message) and support (showing empathy with teachers). This combination actually is quite comforting to teachers because they know what they are trying to achieve and feel that their personal points of view are being considered and heard. Kotter (2012) reminds us that if the change is defined as taking several years and people function in the absence of empathetic pressure, they may indeed delay the start of their work on the initiative, thinking that there isn't an urgency to begin.

To me, the work of initiation is so related to these feelings people may experience early on in the work. Brene Brown (2017) calls the work ahead for anyone involved in deep change "braving the wilderness." She explains that as people are called for greater things, they must both maintain the focus on what is important and have the courage to be individuals and voice their ideas. After compiling interviews of people focusing on the idea of trust, several key actions are critical to her. They include the following (pp. 38–39).

Critical Actions to Help People "Brave the Wilderness" (Brown, 2017)

- Establishing boundaries and asking for clarity around boundaries
- Being reliable to others
- Holding ourselves and others to the standard
- Being benevolent to others
- Behaving according to the community's values
- Withholding judgment
- Creating generosity around actions, ideas, and intentions

I wouldn't call Brown's ideas a checklist but rather a list of considerations, and they have particular significance to the kind of trusting culture that leaders hope to have and develop during the early, stressful work of learning about and considering an important change to schools. In reflecting on her considerations and those of Kotter, Fullan, and Sinek, Brown suggests that the following trust-building actions for leaders fall into place to support early initiation:

- Keep clear on the message and the purpose of the work.
- Provide "gentle" pressure for people to remain focused on the *why* and the *what*.
- Have empathetic conversations with teachers and be open to early concerns they have.
- Communicate clarity about the boundaries of the anticipated change.
- Be tolerant of different points of view, avoiding judgment, while maintaining the focus.

Building Trust Early On

Why Is This Action Important?	What If It Doesn't Happen?
Allows honest conversations about the purpose of the work	People may be initially suspicious of the change.
Encourages open conversations and transparency about the change	People may share their concerns covertly or create dissatisfaction among their peers.
Models a tolerance for varying points of view	People may feel like the change is coupled with an inordinate amount of pressure or a need for conformity.
Creates a professional feeling	Teachers may not feel honored for their hard work and intelligence and begin to distrust the change.

Action #5: Facilitate a Sense of Accomplishment

While teachers may not be actually implementing the change, they will want to visualize where they think they will get started. Often the work of the change will appear overwhelming. This feeling of futility may prevent teachers from making the turn from "learning about it" to "beginning to practice it." Kotter (2012) emphasizes the role of "short-term wins" (p. 126) as critical in reinforcing effort in getting started and providing a clear sense of accomplishment at the very beginning. He believes that short-term wins have three characteristics:

- They are visible and practical.
- They are unambiguous; there can be little argument over their viability.
- They are clearly related to the change effort, although they may appear as small steps.

The implications for leaders, then, are apparent. During early initiation, leaders must engage teachers in their personal deliberations of "where they will get started" on the change so teachers clearly have these short-term goals established. While the effort will be anchored in the long-term purpose, the anticipated teacher actions must feel short term to teachers (Bossidy & Charan, 2009). As each teacher chooses different short-term goals, if those goals are "clearly related to the change effort" (p. 126), they will propel the overall work forward when teachers get started.

Facilitate an Early Sense of Accomplishment

Why Is This Action Important?	What If It Doesn't Happen?
Helps people visualize their first attempts at implementation	People may feel overwhelmed.
Allows people a personalized way to get started	Individual teacher needs are not considered.
Provides the right balance of heat and light	May be viewed as a uniform requirement for the same kind of "getting started" actions, not influenced by individual needs and skills.

Take a Moment

We have taken a deep dive into initiation. It is apparent that initiation of the change is a time that warrants attention. Because of our exploration of this phase and two districts' experiences with it, we are able to reflect on our own practices during this beginning phase:

To what extent do I

- get clear on the purpose of the innovation I want to implement;
- provide a way for teachers to collaboratively help me design a vision which describes the purpose and what we are trying to achieve;
- use the vision to continuously message the purpose before implementation;
- create times for teachers to talk to me about their perception of the change;
- demonstrate understanding of their concerns;
- reinforce the ways I notice their efforts;
- provide well-designed professional learning to give teachers a general understanding of the change;
- reflect on any knowledge gaps that arose during the professional learning and give chances for teachers to individualize their continued learning about the change;
- build trust in how I'm handling the beginning of the change;
- model the kinds of open, trust building behaviors that I want my teachers to demonstrate;
- encourage teachers to begin thinking about "how they will get started" with the change; and
- allow teachers to select their own ways, even if I think they are small or insignificant, to get started?

THE LEADERS OF OUR TWO SCHOOL DISTRICTS INITIATE THE WORK

Kingsport City Schools and the Ashton Unified School District are two distinct examples of varying approaches to the initiation of their changes. After our deep dive into the principles of initiation and its importance to change, it appears to be a good time to look at how each set of leaders handled the initiation of their major change and to understand how their actions related to our five essential actions.

Kingsport City Schools

Kingsport City Schools wanted to "turn the page" and change the version of their instructional coaching program into something more relationship rich and results based. They also wanted to continue to support their principals in deeper instructional ways, seeing the new coaching program as the on-site support for principal understanding of quality teaching and learning. You will remember that in previous years, the former program provided instructional coaches who were assigned to buildings and targeted teachers who were low-performing or considered deficient in curriculum and/or instruction. Brian Cinnamon, assistant director of schools, explains that the former model focused heavily on curriculum knowledge and knowledge of the new state learning standards. Stephanie Potter, former director of professional learning adds, "I'm not even sure how much coaching training they [the former coaches] had, so they may have not been coaching teachers when they thought they were coaching teachers." In the old model, coaches were not seen in a positive light by teachers—in essence, if they showed up at a teacher's door, you knew "you were in trouble."

For all of these reasons, the district wanted a new coaching model that provided the support principals were uniformly requesting and was more welcomed and effective with teachers. So, the district leaders decided that they wanted a more balanced, positive coaching model that simultaneously supported effective curriculum understanding as well as instructional practices. Because the new director of schools saw this as an opportunity to implement a coaching initiative that was more in line with best coaching practices and continue to showcase his district in a positive way, he moved forward with implementing this new coaching program, which was dramatically different from the former one. He was quite specific and strategic in how he saw initiation. He wanted all communication to dispel any resemblance to the old coaching model. He did not mind being very directive in terms of how the program would look and how it would begin. Here are some of his major needs and a few important actions in the approximate order in which they occurred in Kingsport during initiation of instructional coaching:

Clarity of the Vision and Messaging

1. The director felt strongly that in order to initiate a new version of coaching in the district, the new coaches should be called something different. Therefore, he was intentional in terms of the name they were to have. Over a course of several months, he involved a team at the district level who deliberated over the

most important constructs of the new coaching program. As part of that conversation, a new title for the coaches was determined. They were now to be called "instructional design specialists" or InDeS (as they were generally known in Kingsport; pronounced "indies"). All correspondence from that moment on included the new title of the coaches.

2. District personnel were available to visit each school to explain the new version of coaching as instructionally focused and were eager to work with anyone in the school who wanted additional support.

> Purpose of the Change and Clarity of Messaging

3. I was hired to begin long-term consultation with the district and with the newly named InDeS to design, implement, train, and evaluate the new coaching initiative in all 11 schools.

> Need for Knowledge to Alleviate Fears

4. Principals spent time in summer meetings talking about the new version of coaching and how it was to be different from the old version. Early on, they were also updated on what the new coaches were learning and how they were going about their duties.

> Need for Knowledge to Alleviate Fears

5. InDeS were hired to serve each building and were encouraged to establish trust in their buildings by *not* having specific duties at first and building relationships with the wide range of teachers and abilities in their schools.

> Build Trust

6. Principals were asked to create a "contract" with their InDeS in terms of (a) how the InDeS would operate in that school, (b) how they would handle confidential teacher issues and protect teachers from unfair evaluation, and (c) how often the InDeS would meet with the principal. These contracts were disseminated and discussed by each principal at faculty meetings early in the first year of the new instructional coaching initiative.

> Build Trust and Clarity of Messaging

The director's initiation of the instructional coaching change lacked, interestingly, much drama. He had an advantage that other district leaders might not often have. The old connotation of coaching was not popular; teachers resented being "targeted" by the former instructional coaches and some were quite embarrassed to have that forced relationship with their coach. Therefore, the new coaching version seemed more fair, equitable, and transparent to principals, teachers, and the coaches.

The renaming of the coaches seemed like a small action, but the lasting effects of it smoothed the path to implementation. A new name seemed to signal "different and better" to people, and they appeared to embrace it. This contributed to the trust in the new initiative that the director

(Continued)

(Continued)

desired. In effect, the name change buried the old difficult feelings some people had in the former coaching protocols and replaced it with new energy around the "improved" coaching ideals being touted.

There was a considerable amount of communication and clarity about the new initiative, and the director and his staff chose to communicate the major differences most forcefully. Principals were involved early on in the conversation about new instructional coaching; in fact, they had been some of the most vocal in requesting a change to the old program. The principals had a sense that they were helping to design the new program and there was a sense that ownership among them was at a consistently stable level.

The InDeS made it clear to teachers that their roles, at least at first, were to provide whatever assistance the teachers needed. While some of the InDeS complained that they were being asked to help teachers in ways they worried would have little impact on students, they agreed that these "little actions" were powerful in establishing trust with the teachers at their buildings. These small actions also established a sense of accomplishment for both the InDeS and the teachers—while the InDeS may not have been thrilled about some of the things they were being asked to do by the teachers, both they and the teachers felt that they were "doing things" and getting things done.

We will see in the next chapter on implementation that in spite of their efforts to provide any kind of service the teachers were requesting (at first), InDeS were not uniformly welcomed in all classrooms at their schools. Brian Cinnamon reports that "they struggled with how to go about building relationships at schools and how to shift past just providing resources to teachers and move deeper into the work that would make a difference." The InDeS, indeed, felt that they were held to rather narrow means of starting their work at first. This restricted way of beginning their work was clearly communicated and required by the director.

Initiation of this change in Kingsport City Schools took some work and focus. Successfully launching a new initiative, even when the change is welcomed, is never easy. This director and his team seemed to demonstrate quite a bit of savvy in how they knew instructional coaching in his schools could be reimagined and launched.

The Ashton Unified School District

The decision makers in the Ashton Unified School District had studied years of student performance information and had come to the conclusion that a new reading program and material were needed for grades K–5. This decision was led by two groups: (a) the district's school board members who were alarmed at the consistently mediocre student performance and (b) the new superintendent and her curriculum and instruction staff. There was a sense of urgency in this decision. There was a marked lack of consistency and integrity in K–5 reading across the elementary schools. Some teachers in various schools were demonstrating a sophisticated understanding of reading curriculum and instructional strategies, while some teachers in other schools were not. In fact, there was a wide range of teacher knowledge and performance even within the same school. District data verified this wide range of performance in terms of student achievement when matched with teacher competency.

With this issue of uniformly raising the "floor" in terms of curriculum knowledge and instructional strategies in all schools, the new program and materials were purchased for the elementary grades. Leaders' thinking was that the materials would be first initiated and implemented in grades K–2, and then initiated and implemented in grades 3–5 the following year. Here are a few important actions in the approximate order in which they occurred during initiation of instructional coaching.

1. The district leaders felt that the reading need was urgent. They may have also felt that the data, since consistently poor for years, proved the urgent need for an overhaul of the current reading curriculum and practices. It was also assumed that this need was widespread among the teachers and the principals of the elementary schools. When the reading change was communicated, there was some resistance from both teachers and elementary principals for a variety of reasons. The initiation, however, proceeded.

   Clarity of Messaging

2. It may have been assumed that all knew the purpose of the change; however, no initial work was accomplished with the teachers and principals in terms of the desired change and what it would look like in schools (the vision).

   Purpose of the Change

3. Professional learning was held for the K–2 teachers during the summer before implementation, but on a voluntary basis. This took the form of training, led by consultants from the new reading company. In addition, the consultants and a team from the district led training of the instructional coaches on the program. The anticipated outcomes for both coaches and teachers from this training were (a) new knowledge about the "science" of reading, (b) an overview of the various materials the teachers will use, (c) the research behind the practices, and (d) a sense of the pacing

   Need for Knowledge to Alleviate Fears

   (Continued)

(Continued)

of the program to accomplish the goals. In addition, a short training session was conducted for principals (on a voluntary basis) by the consultants of the company. After that, a short series of professional learning opportunities was held for principals during their regular meetings (led by district leaders) to continue to give them a sense of the new program and what to look for in classrooms.

Build Trust and Clarity of Messaging

4. Materials were ordered to support the K–2 implementation; however, not all schools opened the school year with a complete set of materials. Inadequate communication between district leaders and school principals led to frustration in terms of beginning implementation.

Clarity of Messaging

5. School instructional coaches were hired to work in all elementary schools to support quality instruction. These coaches were told to specifically target quality reading instruction using the new K–2 reading materials. Many of them did not have a reading background and/or did not attend the reading training. Teachers were not sure what roles the new instructional coaches were serving.

Build Trust and Provide a Sense of Accomplishment

6. Teachers were asked to begin the new year with a preassessment of the K–2 students to provide information for them to more effectively teach the range of students in classrooms. The preassessment was not reviewed by teachers before its implementation; many teachers were alarmed at the level of the preassessment. Students were generally not successful with the preassessment to the extent that many of them were seen crying in classrooms because of their lack of reading knowledge or skill.

The Ashton Unified School District leaders surely had a reading problem on their hands with the previously used set of curricular materials. Years of student performance information verified this need. It seemed logical to district leaders and school board members to call for an overhaul of the program. Both sets of leaders may have overestimated the agreement they felt teachers and principals would have with the decision. Often, teachers will intellectually understand the need for change but subjectively reject it or be fearful of it. These "illogical fears" may rest in teachers' feelings that they will be inadequate to teach the new program or that the district doesn't appreciate their efforts over the years. There was concern about the new reading program, then, before it was ever fully implemented.

Professional learning to launch the Reach for Reading program was sketchy and inconsistent. According to Debra Olson, a former principal and district leader of the implementation of the program, there were optional sessions for teachers during the spring and summer of 2016. Interestingly, instructional coaches were also being brought to the district the same school year; these coaches were given more extensive training on the reading program. The coaches, then, redelivered this training in a shortened form at the first required in-service day for teachers during the early fall of that year. The quality of this required teacher training hinged on the knowledge and pedagogy ability of the instructional coach. "Coaches at this point were really just one step ahead of teachers in terms of reading pedagogy," explains Joanie Kemper, senior director of teaching and learning. For this reason, the training varied in terms of content and quality. "They (the teachers) got one full day of training for the program. One-half of that day was to see the materials; the other half was to work in collaboration with their fellow teachers to work through the materials and plan together," explains Joanie Kemper. "This was the only training they got during their one day of required in-service that year."

Principals received opportunities to learn about Reach for Reading at first, but those opportunities were on a voluntary basis during that same spring of 2016. "I remember the one I went to when I was still a principal," recalls Debra Olson. "The training wasn't that good—it was not going to hit the mark and I knew already what worked in reading so I didn't pay it much attention." The district did conduct a series of short training sessions in monthly elementary principals' meetings as the first year of implementation proceeded. The superintendent, however, attended some of those principal meetings and became alarmed at the way program initiation and beginning implementation were proceeding; that was the time that Debra Olson (then a principal) was asked to take on dual roles—that of building principal and advisor to the district for the implementation of the program. At this point and until the present, she worked with both principals and instructional coaches to help make them "experts on the science of reading."

Also contributing to the concerns about the program was the student preassessment that teachers were to give the K–2 students during the first fall of the program. Many of the teachers in the Ashton Unified School District are members of their local NEA unit. Diane Connelly, a local union staff member, recalls that "our members began calling our office.

(Continued)

(Continued)

They had been told to give this lengthy preassessment that was part of the new series and when they did, kids began crying. So, a lot of the teachers began calling our office saying that the whole reading change was horrible." To make matters worse, a steering committee to guide the implementation of the K–2 program had already warned district officials not to give the preassessment as it would alarm teachers and make them feel inadequate. Yet, district officials decided to proceed with the assessment. When the word got out that there had been a warning about the preassessment from a committee made up of teachers and yet the district plowed on, there was an immediate negative judgment, at least from a significant number of teachers. These teachers communicated their feelings that no one was understanding their particular issues and how instruction was working in their classrooms.

In Ashton Unified, during this early initiation, there was a feeling that "here we go again" with a new initiative. Because of the lack of a vision (purpose) and communication was either spotty or inconsistent, teachers, coaches, and principals were left to make up their own versions of what the change was and how it would proceed. Was Ashton Unified in trouble at the very start? Yes. Would it be able to recover? We will look at their specific actions to "right their wrongs" in the next chapter and see how the Ashton Unified leaders coped with the issues.

Take a Moment

Both sets of district leaders could justify the changes they initiated, and yet there was varied success between the two districts in how teachers and principals perceived the changes. These two districts provide us great examples of attempts at starting something big. As you think about their experiences, ask yourself the following:

How did the district leaders

- clearly communicate the purpose of the changes;

- invite stakeholders to collaborate with them to design a vision which describes the purpose and what they were trying to achieve;

- create times for teachers to talk to them about their perceptions of the changes that were to come;

- demonstrate understanding of their concerns;

- provide well-designed professional learning to give teachers a general understanding of the change;

- reflect on any knowledge gaps that arose during the professional learning and give chances for teachers to individualize their continued learning about the change;

- build trust about the change and how they were handling it;

- allow time for teachers to begin thinking about "how they will get started" with the change; and

- allow teachers to select their own ways, even if I think they are small or insignificant, to get started?

CHAPTER 3

TROUBLESHOOTING IMPLEMENTATION OVER TIME

Support people to maintain their focus and address the implementation dilemmas that will naturally occur.

Lead for the Long Term and Expect to See a Range of Quality in the Change

When I ask school leaders to consider the idea of schools as both educational and social organizations, I see all sorts of reactions, from nods of understanding to faces of downright rejection of the idea. Yet, so much of change can be explained in terms of people's perceptions and their emotions toward it. When we are initiating a change, there may be a lot of excitement over improving things. Even if there is concern about the change, it may seem like it is in the distant horizon or a little abstract to some, making it easier to bear. We remember that initiation is all of the work *preceding* the actual implementation of the practice.

Things change with implementation. Fullan (2007) reminds us of the differences between initiation and implementation as a contrast between less intricate planning and fewer people issues (during initiation) and more intricate planning and more people issues (during implementation). During implementation, we are talking real change instead of "on paper" planning or decisions. No longer are we just discovering aspects of the change; now, instead, we are relying on that understanding and individual actions to make the change happen. People will be responding to the challenges of how their work looks now. Their personalities, perceptions, feelings of adequacy, and social skills will become a huge focus of the school culture and the leader's work. In implementation, then, change remains as a social construct—in the early part of the change, people are sorting out their feelings about it; during implementation, they are continuing to evolve in their feelings about it as they experience successes and failures. They are also individually sorting out how to make the change in a way that they can professionally and emotionally handle. These complexities of feelings and initial attempts become the leader's focus and work during implementation.

We will define implementation as a people-dependent means of accomplishing the vision or the purpose (Fullan, 2007). It is not simply a matter of "are we accomplishing the practice?" Since effective implementation takes a while and people will respond differently to the work, leaders will see a range of quality as teachers individually work to alter their practice. Because of the time implementation takes and the range of implementation sophistication and effectiveness that we may see over time, the leader's task during this phase is to ask, "*How well are we accomplishing the practice?*" As implementation proceeds, the leader will notice all of the variations she sees as teachers merge the new change into their work.

There are varying opinions about how long implementation will take. I agree with others that it can take a number of years to fully and deeply implement something. I say that because I have seen multitudes of failed projects led by school leaders who believe that the implementation of a new practice should take no more than a year (remember our superintendent who announced "this year's priorities"?).

Embrace the Complexity of Implementation

Inherent in implementation is the idea of long-term persistence of effort and focus, and the sense of getting better and better at something. It is a matter of bringing the new practice from a "novice level" of implementation to a widespread, sophisticated level of implementation over a period of time. Because the schools are organizations of people and there are social influences on them, they will not react in the same way toward the change or implement it uniformly across all colleagues. Hord and Roussin (2013) believe implementation is a very personal action, and they regard this personal range of implementation as the gradual change in behaviors that the implementer is taking in relation to the innovation. Committing to implementation means everyone committing to a long-term, personal relationship with the change. When leaders realize the people-dependence of the work, it helps us understand that the process may not be as smooth as we would like. It is a mistake, then, to think of implementation as simply a matter of fulfilling yearly action plans. We must also take into account and be sensitive to the school's ability (the people within it) to execute those plans (Bossidy & Charan, 2009). Because implementation will be so personal, my belief is that the execution of the implementation plans requires bifocal effort—a relationship-rich *and* results-based focus. Two leadership ideas are critical at this point of change.

The Change Process Is Primarily a People Process. Many leaders have made this mistake of thinking that if the change was effectively planned, then the act of leading implementation should be relatively simple. Those same leaders have probably found effective implementation to be rather elusive. Because schools are highly social organizations, leaders often find themselves faced with dilemmas in the process that are made much more complicated by unique individuals, variations in teacher capacity, and the overall learning and communication culture of the school (Fullan, 2007). Practitioners may discover during implementation that the change is leading to perceptions in the way people are relating to each other or behaving toward each other in the organization (Lawrence, 1969). These are social aspects that, if left unnoticed by the leader, may lead to resistance to the change. Social aspects are particularly dangerous, for they cause change implementers to question whether or not they desire the changes that they may be beginning to see resulting from "doing" the change (Powell & Kusama-Powell, 2015).

In addition, individuals faced with the change will react to it in part due to the perceived degree of change they are anticipating. The greater the perceived degree and depth of the change, the greater the amount of danger that the leader will feel as he or she attempts to orchestrate the change.

In thinking back to the previous chapter, we remember that during the start of the change, or initiation, people want (a) as much information as they can get, (b) to know how the change will personally affect them, and (c) to understand the driving purpose of the change. As we shift into actually practicing the change, the kinds of "people issues" will evolve. Many of the teachers will feel that they have enough information to get started. Their need to know how the change will affect them, however, may shift from personal worries to concerns about implementation efficiency. In other words, during implementation, the issues now may revolve around implementing the change smoothly, effectively, and efficiently rather than the personal toll the change may have on them.

The focus on the purpose is just as important during implementation as it was when starting the innovation. The leader must look at the purpose as being a continuous thread that he hopes to weave for the teachers doing the work. In fact, when teachers are actually beginning to use the innovation or make the change, they may have trouble with it. The point of implementation uneasiness may be the most important time for leaders to make sure people are reminded of the *why*.

Create and Implement Plans That Are Firm and Flexible, Directive and Collaborative. The most effective implementation leader will use a combination of "balancing factors that do not apparently go together— simultaneous simplicity-complexity, looseness-tightness, strong direction-user participation, bottom-up/top-downness, fidelity-adaptivity, and evaluation-nonevaluation" (Fullan, 2007, p. 86). "The organization can execute only if the leader's heart and soul are immersed in the company. . . . The leader has to be engaged personally and deeply in the business. Execution requires a comprehensive understanding of a business, its people, and its environment" (Bossidy & Charan, 2009, p. 24).

Although the change may have been initiated by the district or even at the state or provincial level, the actual work of "making the change happen" takes place in schools. Thus, this constant blend of loose-tight, fidelity-adaptivity, pressure-support will be most useful at the school level and is the responsibility of the leader and all of the school teachers and staff who work there. During implementation, individuals are attempting to "work out their own meaning" (Fullan, 2007, p. 123). When these individuals feel that they can develop their own ways to adapt the change into their practice and still hold true to the standards and the purpose of the change, they will begin to have more and more clarity about the change and how it is intended (Fullan, 2007).

The pressure, then, that teachers feel during implementation should be purposeful and distinct, not be viewed as an act of simply bullying for compliance. "It will be effective only under conditions that allow them (teachers) to react, to form their own position, to interact with other implementers, to obtain assistance, to develop new capacities, and so on" (Fullan, p. 123).

Leadership Essential Actions During Implementation

The same five essential leader actions that were critical during initiation are equally important during implementation. Yet, because of our long-term view of sustained change, the nature of these actions will adjust to specific needs and dilemmas that implementers face as they are attempting to make the change successful and lasting.

Action #1: Strategically Communicate the Purpose/Vision.

Our assumption is that at this point of long-term change, the purpose of the change has been both collaboratively developed and articulated, most likely through the vision. The vision serves as the guiding light and the synthesizer for all of the change work being proposed and accomplished at the school. During the initiation of the change, the purpose and vision helped teachers remain focused while they were learning about the change and wondering how it would affect them. When it is time to begin implementation, there is no rest for leaders who feel that they have successfully created and communicated the vision for the work. At the point of implementation, "attention is focused on the processes and tasks of using the innovation and the best use of the information and resources. Issues of efficiency, organizing, managing, schedule, and time demands are utmost" (Hall & Hord, 2001).

I believe that during implementation, the work becomes "real" and the problems are more impactful because they hit at the heart of the teachers' workday. Leaders may begin to hear complaints such as "we can't get it all done within the day" or "I don't have the right materials to teach my kids" or "my students aren't handling this new program very well." These are signals of what Fullan (2001) calls the "implementation dip." The implementation dip is really a dip in both individual teacher performance and teacher confidence as he encounters the realities of making a change happen that may require new understandings or new skills (Fullan, 2001). When these issues become central among teachers, leaders know that their obligation is to find opportunities to re-communicate the purpose of the change and invite deeper, more transparent communication about the practical difficulties that teachers are facing. In other words, the leader's first inclination might be to try to avoid the implementation issues that are popping up; however, my suggestion is that is the perfect time

Leaders should *lean into* the issues as a chance to revisit why the change is needed at this time and to reinforce teachers' great efforts.

Communicating the Purpose/Vision During Implementation

Why Is This Action Important?	What If It Doesn't Happen?
Redirects people to the purpose of the work and serves to reassure that the effort will be worth it	People may, over time, lose the clarity and the compelling nature of the *why* they experienced during initiation.
Maintains a focus, boosts energy, and builds individual confidence	People may fall back into a fragmented way of thinking of all they are doing and lose the purpose for any of their multiple initiatives.
Invites transparent conversations among leaders and teachers, allowing the real issues to surface and be addressed	People may feel that there is no vehicle to discuss how the purpose is not being actualized during implementation.

for leaders to *lean into* the issues as a chance to revisit why the change is needed at this time and to reinforce teachers' great efforts.

Action #2: Listen and Be Empathetic to Concerns

Reminding people of the purpose during implementation is incredibly important. This focus is not only maintained by the leader's words and actions; it is also reinforced by the leader's willingness to authentically listen to the issues that are perceived as frequent and serious. During implementation, practitioners will usually be eager to talk about the change and be honest about the concerns they have. The concerns feel very legitimate to teachers. The knowledge about how staff members are reacting to the change gives leaders insights as to how to address the more significant and consistent concerns. The listening to the "bad stuff" may seem counterintuitive to us. We usually like to focus on the positive aspects of changes in schools in an attempt to maintain energy. Yet, if there is listening and then actions to address the concerns, odds are that teachers will tend to stay with the change and be more motivated to work toward full, deep implementation (Hall & Hord, 2001).

This act of listening need not be long or complicated. The listening approach I find most effective during implementation is generally unrehearsed, informal, one-on-one, and supportive. Commonly called the one-legged interview (as its duration is roughly equivalent to the time a person can stand on one foot; Hall & Hord, 2001), it is a short verbal conversation between the leader and the individual teacher during which the teacher shares "honest reactions about what he thinks is going on—and going wrong" with the change (Tomlinson & Murphy, 2015, p. 115).

The mechanics of the one-legged conversation are rather simple. Generally following this order, the leader

1. asks the teacher if he or she has a minute to talk;

2. names the specific change and asks the teacher to think about his or her own experiences with implementing it;

3. invites the teacher to tell him or her all of her worries or concerns in full;

4. remains attentive and exercises probing, restating, and summarizing but not fixing the issues; and

5. thanks the teacher for his or her honest dialogue and promises to use the information to help support the innovation in a more successful way

The one-legged conversation has multiple goals. First of all, it is a chance for the leader to demonstrate empathy. Because the leader does not immediately jump to a solution but instead probes and attempts to understand the issue better, the teacher receives the message that his or her opinion matters and that the leader values that perspective. Second, the conversation is a chance for the leader to actually *learn* what is happening when teachers are trying to use the innovation. The one-legged conversation is often most useful when the leader conducts multiple conversations with different teachers within a relatively narrow span of time. If multiple conversations are held, the synthesis of the conversations will become the leader's formative assessment of the progress of implementation at that particular time. There may be patterns of issues that emerge if the leader asks several teachers to engage in these conversations. The issues and the leader's understanding of them will focus him or her on possible solutions, and the chance of those solutions meeting the demands of the issues are heightened because the problems have been honestly described by the people who are attempting the work. Third, the one-legged conversation sends a direct message that while there are issues, the change will not go away. The leader's message during these conversations is to inquire about the problems that are occurring. The promise given in the close of the conversation is that the leader will use what he or she learned to better address his or her support for the innovation—not that the problems may cause the innovation to go away.

By not immediately solving the problems, leaders are demonstrating their willingness to listen and understand, elevating the teacher's concerns.

I find that my most effective one-legged conversations occur when I do not attempt to immediately solve the issue the teacher is discussing. The act of *not* fixing the issues during the short interviews may be equally effective for you. By not immediately solving the problems, leaders are demonstrating their willingness to listen and understand, elevating the teacher's concerns. If the concerns or worries fall into patterns, the leader's responses will address the concerns and allow the teachers to move forward in their work (Tomlinson & Murphy, 2015).

Listening to Early Concerns During Implementation

Why Is This Action Important?	What If It Doesn't Happen?
Helps form an empathetic partnership between the leader and teachers	People may feel that they can't talk about their worries with leaders.
Reinforces the efforts people are making to embrace the change	People may feel that their efforts are "not good enough" and harshly judge their own competence.
Gives leaders insights as to what the problems might be or what people need at this time	Leaders might make mistakes in assuming they understand how to support people unless they ask and listen.
Provides open communication in which both the leader and the implementer explore the issues	The change runs the risk of being viewed as the leader's change or that the leader is detached from the practical issues of implementation.

Action #3: Provide Pathways for People to Acquire What They Need to Be Good at It

As teachers move into their implementation of the new practices, they will need a varying set of professional support if they are to continue to grow in their expertise and implement the change at more effective levels. Three key "truths" make sense (Tomlinson & Murphy, 2015):

1. While training was important during initiation to allow teachers to grasp a basic understanding of the change and the principles behind it, training is not generally useful in showing teachers *how* to implement the change. In addition, simply providing an overload of training at the very beginning of initiation and then not providing additional professional support during the critical phase of implementation amounts to malpractice.

2. Teachers' practices and needs will vary along a wide range of confidence, competence, and implementation success.

3. Professional learning must demonstrate a differentiated approach over time and become more job-embedded, relating to each teacher's evolving emotions and implementation needs.

As teachers work to implement the change, the most valuable professional learning will occur at schools, be more informal, and will happen "just in time." This kind of professional learning is guided by the results that teachers are seeking and the kind of natural collaboration that will typically solve their day-to-day issues. Professional learning to support implementation may look a lot like this—teachers simply finding each other to work and problem solve—and this doesn't match our more formalized idea of "good" professional learning. Yet, this kind of teacher-to-teacher work is professional learning that is just as valuable as training was in initiation; in this case, the professional learning adjusts and differentiates to address the kinds of needs that teachers will now have. Called "job-embedded," it is informal, strategic, and "deliberate and focused, but in a way that may be unfamiliar to school leaders" (Tomlinson & Murphy, 2015, p. 68).

Powerful, job-embedded, school-based professional learning builds "interdependence" among teachers, an essential concept if the change will last (Little, 2008). As teachers work to implement the change in meaningful ways, they will be benefitted if they begin to rely on each other a bit and learn from each other as they work with the change. As Little (2008) reminds us, "The ability of a group to both influence individual practice and collective practice is contingent on aims held in common. Without some kind of foundational commitment to ambitious kinds of practice, the likelihood of the group having influence on that kind of practice is probably small" (p. 54). Little's words reinforce the idea that the group of teachers will positively influence each other's practice if they continue to understand what they are trying to achieve and share ways to achieve it. This "joint work" (Little, 2008), which is shared by teachers, holds them together as they dialogue about the practical issues and reminds leaders why it is so important to continue to communicate the purpose in the implementation phase.

Therefore, there is a huge need for continued professional learning during the implementation phase. The goal of creating professional learning for teachers at this point is that it will be practical, job-embedded, and will create a forum to address implementation issues. Any of the following professional learning designs might have promise for the leader interested in supporting implementation after the training has occurred. All of these designs take place at the school and are listed here in no particular sequence or importance:

- Teachers work together to write lesson plans.
- Teachers study the curriculum standards together and select materials that best address those standards.
- Teachers teach a concept, then collect samples of student work and collaboratively analyze them.
- Teachers analyze real case studies of students who are struggling and determine promising practices to address these struggles.
- Teachers watch an instructional coach teach a concept and then debrief.
- Teachers watch each other teach an instructional concept and then debrief.
- Teachers set an instructional goal together and then assess to see if they met their goals.
- Teachers immerse themselves in the program and experience it as though they were the students, then write lesson plans together.
- Teachers meet informally in faculty meetings to address the types of issues they are having with the implementation of the change.
- Teachers meet an additional time other than their planning time to focus specifically on the implementation of the change and troubleshoot.
- Teachers dive deeper into the change by selecting a book for a book study and then committing to actions they learned, sharing the results of those actions with each other.

If the school leader can find and arrange the time, teachers are most willing to problem solve in order to sustain their efforts for the change. They will even be happy to select the job-embedded professional learning design that would work best for them. So much of job-embedded, implementation-focused professional learning is so informal that the leaders might not think of it to be valid. But in a culture of exchange, trust, and focus, even the most informal conversations between two dedicated teachers can be profound.

Creating Pathways for People to Acquire What They Need to Implement Well

Why Is This Action Important?	What If It Doesn't Happen?
Focuses on the actual work and the "doing" of the change	People may feel that they have been abandoned or inadequately prepared for the change.
Acknowledges that informal, job-embedded designs best support teachers when they are doing the work	Without the ongoing support, the initial issues teachers face may force them to abandon the change.
Connects teachers with each other as informal resources	It further isolates teachers and creates a lack of interdependence.

Action #4: Build Their Trust in You, the Work, and Each Other

Remember that Brene Brown (2017) calls the work ahead for anyone involved in deep change "braving the wilderness." She explains that as people are "called for greater things," they must both (a) maintain the focus on what is important and (b) have the courage to be individuals and voice their ideas. During implementation, as teachers are attempting to adapt the change to their own practices, they will be met with "wilderness challenges" on a daily basis. While building trust in the initiation phase focused primarily on the "why are we doing it" and "what is it," trust will continue to be built during implementation by also providing ways the implementers can discuss the *how* and by encouraging individuals implementing the change to remain partners with leaders and each other in the process.

This does not mean, however, that leaders should consider the *why* as something people will remember over time. As people begin doing the work of the change, they will focus a lot of their energy and attention on creating efficient ways to absorb the change into their practices. The refocusing of their attention toward the *how* may allow the *why* to grow fuzzy over time (Sinek, 2009). When people are so involved in the daily challenges of the work, it is so easy to lose the purpose for it; it builds confidence, trust, and continuity in the work if leaders continue to choose creative times to reinforce the purpose and acknowledge teachers' efforts.

Trust is also reinforced when leaders and colleagues choose to have informal conversations with each other while doing the work. As we have said before, change in schools is accomplished by individuals;

as these individuals begin to express their ideas and seek their voice (Brown, 2017), they will want to share their successes and their worries. During implementation, teachers are seeking to adapt, not adopt, the change into their practices. Each individual will have different challenges and successes, and he or she will want to see dialogue about the change with both the leader and their colleagues. Implementation is all about building a culture of "execution" (Bossidy & Charan, 2009). "You cannot have an *execution culture* without robust dialogue—one that brings reality to the surface through openness, candor, and informality. Robust dialogue makes an organization effective in gathering information, understanding the information, and reshaping it to produce decisions" (p. 102).

These conversations, if transparent, will invariably focus on different points of view and approaches, with the inherent idea of uncovering varying ideas with an open mind. The act of opening up deeper dialogue during implementation may seem like a dangerous leadership tactic during implementation. Many leaders will just want to keep their heads down and work toward "fidelity of implementation," which they may interpret as "everybody follow the rules and do it uniformly." I am sure that is not the wisest choice. If leaders discount the legitimate worries and points of view (even new ideas about how to do it), they will be actually demeaning the professionalism of teachers and undermining that culture of collaborative execution. I believe that if teachers understand the *why*, and feel they have the information they need (the *what*), almost all will commit to implementation over time—if they have an avenue to voice their ideas within a culture of safety. Leaders, then, build trust in the work, in them, and in each other by not being "trapped by preconceptions or armed with a private agenda" (Bossidy & Charan, 2009, p. 102). To put it simply, the leader's job in implementation is not to coerce compliance or "sell" the innovation. Trust will be built in the change and motivation will be reinforced, even in difficult implementation times, by wanting to hear the issues while remaining focused on the eventual goal. (See the idea of the one-legged conversation earlier in this chapter as a vehicle for listening, problem solving, and trust building.)

While building trust during implementation may seem challenging, it is the glue that will hold the culture together as it endures predictable "how to do it" challenges. By continuing to focus on the purpose, the leader will be continuing the challenge; by focusing on dialogue, the leader will demonstrate high-support (Tschannen-Moran, 2004). "Trustworthy leadership shows the way through example and by providing the resources, norms, and structures for others to be trustworthy as well" (p. 185).

Building Trust During Implementation

Why Is This Action Important?	What If It Doesn't Happen?
Facilitates honest conversations about the purpose of the work and invites dialogue about the day-to-day dilemmas, providing the pressure and support people need	People may feel that their legitimate ideas and voices are silenced, leading to dissatisfaction and a loss of motivation.
Ensures compliance to the change while providing a pathway for discontent and perhaps solution finding	People may share their concerns covertly or create dissatisfaction among their peers.
Creates times for collegial collaboration that encourage idea sharing and problem solving and create trust in the work and in each other	When implementation becomes difficult, people may abandon their effort if they feel there is no way to problem solve with others.

Action #5: Facilitate a Sense of Accomplishment

While the purpose of the change will be motivating and inspiring, the *fulfillment* of the purpose should be enhanced teacher and student accomplishment. Often a change is considered at the district or school level because of low student performance, which is an obvious goal. It's essential that the implementation of the change will focus on that ultimate student performance goal; however, during day-to-day work, the leader will want to make sure implementers see incremental progress—based on more formative goals. Higher student performance is certainly a big dream, but during day-to-day implementation, a focus on the ultimate achievement may be dangerous if "people become so caught up in big dreams that they don't manage the current reality" (Kotter, 2012, p. 122). A sole focus on the ultimate goal may be too remote and too overwhelming. During implementation, then, the implementers will need to not only be focused on the big dreams but also experience short-term wins. These short-term wins are critical if the focus is to be maintained and the big dream eventually realized.

As Kotter (2012) describes, short-term wins are not gimmicks; they are legitimate ways to show evidence that individual efforts are paying off. People are motivated in part by "mastery" (Pink, 2009), which is defined as a sense that they are reaching a big goal by skillfully incorporating steady, visible, small actions. Because impactful change will prove to be complicated and take some time to get fully and effectively in place, complex skills aren't simply mastered within a single day.

We already know that adults (and children, by the way) don't suddenly acquire a body of knowledge and skills to implement an important change after adequate training (Shapiro, 2011). Therefore, during implementation, the idea of recognizing and promoting short-term wins has some science to support it.

If short-term wins are critical and individuals will want to experience these short-term wins, it makes sense that not all of the individuals implementing the change will have exactly the same knowledge, skills, and habits of mind to experience the same kind and number of short-term wins. Vygotsky's work (1980, 1986) identified the progression from novice to expert or master as a relationship that exists between the current state of that individual's knowledge and skill and the kind of support that can result in the deeper implementation of this knowledge and skills. The leader, then, must be attuned to the kinds of support and experiences that will "move each individual teacher" forward to experience short-term wins. He must be willing to differentiate that support and experiences, because the individuals doing the work are not all the same and do not need the same experiences to move them to greater mastery.

If people do not experience these regular short-term wins, the whole work and the ultimate outcomes are in danger. While Bossidy and Charan (2009) focus their work on the business world, their warning is relevant to us in the business of school leadership.

> Balancing the short run with the long run is thus a critical part of a strategic plan. Most plans address what a company has to do between the time the plan is drawn up and the time it is supposed to yield peak results. Because they focus on the beginning and the ultimate end, they may not capitalize on short-term wins that make the peak yields possible. A plan that doesn't deal with the near-term issues of costs, productivity, and people makes getting from here to there unacceptably risky—and often impossible. (p. 199)

Facilitate a Sense of Accomplishment During Implementation

Why Is This Action Important?	What If It Doesn't Happen?
Helps people feel a sense of accomplishment and efficacy	The big dream may seem so far away that it is unattainable, leading to resistance or a lack of action.

Overtly aligns the short-term wins with the big dream and helps people see that the sequence of work is pointed in the right direction	Short-term wins may not be seen as connected to the big dream or goal.
Provides teachers with differentiated support and experiences so they can feel individualized short-term wins	They may feel left out because of the presumption that all should proceed with implementing the change in the same way.
Allows for individual teachers to continue to feel they are a part of a larger community, achieving the purpose	It fragments the work and the message.

Take a Moment

As we did in the initiation chapter, this seems like a good time to reflect on how we handle the challenging issues of long-term implementation. Consider these questions.

To what extent do I

- find creative ways to message the purpose (vision of the change) so people remain focused and motivated;

- use the vision to invite open, honest conversations about the issues teachers are having when implementing the change;

- help teachers see how their day-to-day actions are purposeful and help us achieve the vision;

- create regular times for teachers to share their concerns about the change;

- demonstrate my understanding about their implementation concerns;

- listen more and talk less when the subject centers on the change we are seeking;

- use the one-legged conversation technique to learn about the issues and build trust;

- find times and ways for teachers to informally share their implementation successes;

- find times for teachers to work together to troubleshoot their implementation issues or dilemmas;

(Continued)

(Continued)

- focus my conversation on their practical issues while maintaining a steady eye on the vision;

- encourage teachers to be open and honest with me regarding their implementation mindset;

- create ways to acknowledge the short-term wins; and

- differentiate my support of teachers so they can engineer their own ways to move forward with implementation?

THE LEADERS OF OUR TWO DISTRICTS IMPLEMENT THEIR WORK

Each set of district leaders felt the need for a change that they considered worthy of years of work, initiating the work from the top down. Let's look at how each set of leaders attempted to move from initiation into implementation and transfer the responsibility to the schools to enact their changes. Let's also see how leadership actions in both districts either demonstrated or didn't demonstrate our five essential actions as they entered implementation.

Kingsport City Schools

For many legitimate reasons, Kingsport City Schools leaders wanted a new coaching model that provided better support of instruction and more assistance to principals, who were uniformly requesting additional school-based help. The leadership initiated a more balanced, positive coaching model that simultaneously supported effective curriculum understanding as well as instructional practices that could be invaluable to the principals of their 11 schools. The new director of schools was heavily involved in not only communication about the new coaching initiative but also how it would look in the schools. Generally speaking, the initiation of the coaching program appeared to unfold smoothly. The titles of the new coaches were changed to communicate a different approach, principals were involved in gaining information about the program, and the new coaches were immersed in professional learning to support not only their knowledge of curriculum and instruction but also their coaching skills. In addition, after the coaches were assigned to buildings, they were asked to create and adhere to a "coaching contract" between them and their principals. The intent of the coaching contract was for each principal and his or her coach to be really clear on what the coaching partnership would look like at each school. This partnership contract was shared at every school, and requests were made for teacher feedback regarding the contract and the InDeS' responsibilities.

All of this preparatory work evolved into implementation as the coaches were assigned to buildings and the school year started. Here are some important implementation milestones and challenges as the coaches began their work at schools:

1. Coaches began their work by assisting teachers in a variety of ways, including some assistance that coaches personally felt would probably not be impactful. For instance, coaches were asked by teachers to help sort materials, find additional materials, and so on. While the teachers felt that the coaches could solve these small issues, the coaches were eager to begin work with teachers on deeper concepts such as curriculum understanding or the implementation of new instructional practices. This disconnect between the coaches' idea of the work in which they would be involved and the teachers' immediate needs (especially at the start of the school year) caused some anxiety and concern among the coaches. These concerns were voiced at the monthly coaches' meetings, and coaches were encouraged to notice their short-term wins while knowing that their work would eventually reach the curriculum or instructional work they desired.

   Clarity of Messaging and Sense of Accomplishment

2. It appeared that early on, principals still had limited knowledge about the function of the coaches, and they put some coaches in situations that the coaches felt did not align with their duties. As principals attended monthly meetings, they were asked to share how they were using the coaches, and district leaders reinforced effective ways to use the coaches.

   Purpose of the Change and Provide Ongoing Learning

3. Coaches continued to meet with district leaders on a monthly basis during the first year; there was much work done to build internal trust among the coaches by sharing ideas and skills with each other. When there was an internal conflict among the coaches, it was surfaced and district leaders engaged in dialogue with coaches until the resolution.

   Listen to Concerns and Build Trust

(Continued)

(Continued)

Sense of
Accomplishment

4. The director of schools asked coaches to keep logs of how they were spending their time on a biweekly basis. These logs were compiled and the information was analyzed by coaches and district leaders to see if the teacher requests for support were shifting away from "meaningless things" to curricular or instructional help. When the data were analyzed and compared from the start of the year to the end of the year, it revealed that shift.

Clarity of Messaging

5. Coaches were asked in their monthly meetings to target two high-performing teachers and directly work with them. This strategic decision reinforced the message that the purpose of this coaching model was to provide support to all in the schools, not just the individuals who were in the most need.

Provide
Ongoing Learning

6. Quarterly professional learning sessions were held with coaches (conducted by an external consultant) so they could continue to learn about coaching, practice the skills in a safe setting, and solve their implementation dilemmas. Elementary coaches began meeting on their own in addition to the time with the entire coaching group. During these elementary meetings, the four coaches targeted specific elementary curricular issues.

Provide
Ongoing Learning

7. District leaders determined that during year two, the external consultant would also meet regularly with the principals to ensure coordination of efforts, mutual learning, and dialogue about successful actions with their coaches.

Sense of
Accomplishment

8. Multiple coaching assessment measures were selected and the information was gathered to determine how the overall coaching initiative was progressing. These multiple program assessment measures included 24 individual teacher case studies of instructional accomplishment. All measures were combined, interpreted, and communicated to the board of trustees, principals, teachers, and coaches.

These actions and results look impressive, and yet in Kingsport, the implementation of the new coaching initiative was not perfect. The fact that principals, even in beginning implementation, still had a cursory understanding of the coaches' duties (even after spending quite a bit of time learning about the coaches' intended roles) was frustrating. Brian Cinnamon sheds light on the district leaders' response to this lack of understanding. He explains, "So we felt that we needed to stay with our design and create the capacity of the individuals who were doing key work (the principals) to support the coaches. We had to stick to what we felt was the role of the InDeS." So, instead of letting the coaching role "drift" toward something unintentional, the principals were engaged in ongoing training and dialogue about coaching roles and successes. This ongoing work with principals continued into the second and third years.

The coaches experienced some issues as well. They had high levels of energy and were eager to help teachers in profound ways. There was a general feeling of impatience among them when some initial constraints were put on them by district leaders. "InDeS wanted to get their feet in the doors but they were prohibited from some duties at the schools (such as leading the professional learning community time of grade levels or departments). That was frustrating," Stephanie Potter explains. The director of schools, however, felt strongly about narrowing the focus of the coaches at first—he continued to feel strongly that the implementation of the coaching initiative was helping to shape their brand, and he did not allow anything to get in the way of that perception.

The coaches began to sense the early fruits of their labor when they were asked to keep voluminous amounts of data regarding their duties. When they reviewed the compiled data and saw that indeed their roles were shifting from inconsequential to more impactful (over time), they were thrilled and eager to dig even deeper into their work. At first, they complained about the record keeping for this data collection, but district leaders remained firm but empathetic to their issues, reminding them of the rationale for the data collection. This seemed to satisfy the coaches.

As principals were engaged more and more as partners in the coaching work, they were introduced to coaching knowledge and skills and were asked to also practice these skills in their schools. Some of the principals treated this additional professional learning as "something extra" and were not as enthusiastic about the work. This may have been because they did not see the purpose for the additional professional learning. Because of principals' reactions, district leaders focused the professional learning on tangible products, such as the development of school vision statements and the incorporation of the coaching support into their yearly "change plans" to accomplish their visions. When the emphasis shifted from learning about coaching and school improvement to the application of that knowledge, principals were generally reassured and found the processes to be valuable.

At the date of this book's publication, the Kingsport coaching program is in its fourth year of implementation. School achievement results have been encouraging. In the school year 2018–2019, 6 of the 11 schools were

(Continued)

(Continued)

recognized by the state as having the highest achievement quotient when demographics, economic diversity, and student performance metrics are used. The coaches continue to meet on a monthly basis. Principals are still utilizing the coaches in impactful ways. The Kingsport City Schools board of trustees has passed district budgets for three additional years, which include funding for the full complement of coaches. The culture of the schools appears to have embraced the InDeS with eager arms. There is virtually no conversation among teachers or leaders about "the way we used to do coaching." In the next chapter, we will see what district leaders did to ensure that the initiative would continue to last and produce fruit.

The Ashton Unified School District

The decision to implement a new reading program in grades K–5 in the Ashton Unified School District was led by two groups: (a) the district's school board members who were alarmed at the consistently mediocre student performance and (b) the new superintendent and her curriculum and instruction staff. There was a sense of urgency in this decision. The new program and materials were purchased, and district leaders planned for the implementation of the program in grades K–2 only during the first year, with grades 3–5 brought on in the next school year. The Ashton leaders' thinking was that by phasing the reading program in, there would be less turmoil and the first year could provide a learning year for leaders so the implementation of grades 3–5 could proceed even smoother. Remember that the Ashton leaders' initiation of the change was full of issues, which became quite paralyzing even before the materials were being used. Leaders struggled to "get ahead" of the issues and to focus on the purpose of the change; and yet, that purpose seemed to get lost for many of the people. The following illustrate some major decisions and challenges that the Ashton Unified School District leaders faced as they moved from initiation to full implementation in the first year for grades K–2.

Build Trust and Provide a Sense of Accomplishment

1. The teachers had participated in summer training regarding the reading program, and yet all of the materials were not at buildings until the start of that school year. For many teachers, the first time they saw the reading materials was on the first day of school with their students or during their required in-service day.

Listen to Concerns

2. As the district was moving from initiation and preparation to beginning implementation, district leaders made the decision that it would be helpful for K–2 teachers to have current reading

information about their students. As a result, in the fall of
that first year, all K–2 teachers were instructed to administer a
preassessment to their students in order to get this beginning
information on student knowledge and skills. During the
administration of this preassessment, many students cried and
became visibly upset. Teachers also had emotional reactions and
began contacting district officials to ask for permission not to give
the assessment. District officials did not amend their decision and
did not allow any variation with the preassessment (they were
concerned about program fidelity). Many teachers were furious
and began attending school board meetings to complain about
the preassessment and the general way district leaders were "not
listening." Many teachers also contacted their local education
association for intervention.

3. As implementation began in K–2, instructional coaches' roles
   were altered to focus solely on reading for those grades. This
   role change occurred with little knowledge or collaboration with
   coaches. In addition, many coaches felt ill-prepared to support the
   new reading program as they had not participated in the training
   or did not have a reading background.

   Clarity of Messaging and Provide Ongoing Learning

4. Since teachers had very little personal preparation time before
   school started, they felt thrown into the program and its many
   components. They struggled with the implementation of all of
   the components although they were told by district officials to
   implement the entire program. The entire implementation felt
   like, in my thinking, they were "building the plane while flying it."

   Sense of Accomplishment

5. Principals were asked to work with a separate consultant on
   what good reading looks like in the classroom. They began
   participating in "learning walks" designed to watch teachers
   teach reading to give principals a sense of the implementation
   of quality reading practices. Teachers were not informed of the
   purpose of the classroom visits. They saw them as punative and
   evaluative. The learning walks continued.

   Clarity of Messaging

6. There was no district-led conversation or development of school-
   based ways to support teachers and encourage them to work
   together for better implementation. Many principals felt that if the
   teachers had summer training, that was sufficient. Teachers were
   forced to participate in additional planning meetings with their
   colleagues but questioned the rationale of this decision. They

   Clarity of Messaging and Sense of Accomplishment

(Continued)

(Continued)

were not informed as to the purpose of these meetings or the products that were to come from them.

Clarity of Messaging and Provide Ongoing Learning

7. The district responded to teachers' complaints that the reading program was overwhelming and that they were unable to fit all of the activities into their limited teaching schedules. The district response was to help teachers by creating "priority plans," district-produced pacing guides intended to show teachers how to use their time to teach the reading materials effectively. The priority plans were to be used in conjunction with the materials. The plans were distributed to teachers in mid-fall of the first year with no professional learning to support them. The priority plans included minute-to-minute prescriptions of how to teach an idea and for how long. Teachers reacted to these additional plans by feeling that the district was further constraining their academic freedom by providing a tight recipe and allowing no variation from that recipe.

Listen to Concerns and Build Trust

8. After contract negotiations and tense meetings with local education association representatives, the decision was made to draft an agreement between the association and the district that gave teachers some academic freedom in the classrooms. In addition, an outside consultant (me) was hired to help the district "save" the implementation and guide the district into a smoother implementation of the program in grades 3–5.

Listen to Concerns and Build Trust

9. A reading "steering committee" was formed and began to meet regularly with me to learn about effective implementation, design a way to assess progress, problem solve, and communicate to teachers.

Provide Ongoing Learning and Clarity of Messaging

10. Members of the steering committee generated a vision for the program that articulated the purpose. This vision was shared with principals and teachers at school meetings.

Sense of Accomplishment

11. I began working with the steering committee to design a program assessment framework, to be implemented in each quarter, and collect informal data on how the program is progressing.

Build Trust and Sense of Accomplishment

12. The steering committee met at each quarter to review and interpret the program implementation data and to make some recommendations and adjustments to expectations.

13. A task force of teachers was created to make changes in the priority plans so they could be more useful to teachers.

Build Trust

In the Ashton Unified School District, then, initiation of the new reading program was inconsistent, and the preparation for implementation was not perceived as well-planned. Materials were not delivered on time, instructional coaches were unclear as to their roles, and principals were ill-equipped to lead the implementation at their buildings. As they moved into the school year and implementation began, things appeared to get worse. "It started to fall apart early," reflects Debra Olson, former elementary principal and now coordinator of the project. "Teachers didn't know what to teach and how to teach it." Conner Austen, Ashton teacher and local education association union leader, concurs: "By the end of October of that first year, things were pretty grim. Implementation was failing so miserably that there was a reaction by making the coaches 'reading coaches' and implementing priority plans. Times were so structured for teachers and there was a feeling that this was just another issue of layering on (piling on) change after change."

Diane Connelly agrees. "It was too much too soon. Coaches were brought into it and teachers did not know their role in it, the preassessment was inappropriate, the summer training felt inadequate to some, grade-level planning was being prescribed, and the whole program seemed rigid and prescriptive." Representatives of the local union contacted district officials to share the concerns they were hearing, and some district leaders were eager to hear the problems and generate solutions. There was a feeling, however, that these good conversations and problem-solving sessions didn't "trickle down" to the schools, as Connelly put it. "Everything was lost in translation, and implementation of the program across schools began to look inconsistent."

The preassessment that teachers were required to give their students during the fall of the first year was intended to give teachers a baseline of their students' skills in reading. The effect of the preassessment was just the opposite. "The preassessment was a disaster, teachers were making students do it, and the principals began coming to principals' meetings complaining about it and other aspects of the program," recalls Debra Olson. "[The superintendent] was at one of those meetings and also attended a coaches' meeting, and she was horrified. That is when she asked me to step in [from my principal position] and help during this early part of implementation."

(Continued)

(Continued)

The priority plans, district pacing guides, were created early on to assist in implementation; but they were developed after the beginning of the program, not in conjunction with the initiation of the program. The intent of the priority plans was to give teachers an idea of how to incorporate the required elements of exceptional reading within their scheduled reading time. There were two sets of plans created. One set was called "core plans," which were for most schools where reading achievement was average or above average. The other plans, called "core plus plans," were created to give teachers in the lower-performing or Title schools some additional strategies and guidance. Teachers, early in the implementation, actually requested this guidance from the district in terms of pacing. Debra Olson explains, "Teachers said, we don't know what to teach. The priority plans were built first for the Title schools and then for other schools. They were distributed about mid-year that first year."

The effects of Ashton's efforts to provide additional pacing assistance were unanticipated by district leaders. There was training about the priority plans, but again that was handled by instructional coaches at their respective schools. "The training was for one day. That wasn't enough; and we didn't do a good job of getting them (the teachers) ready for all of this. It was fast and furious, but something had to change," said Debra Olson as she recalled the development of the plans. Although there was some teacher request for the pacing guides, most teachers had issues with the guides when given to them. Some teachers liked the guidance, and yet many teachers felt that this was another way that the district was taking away their ability to use centers for instruction and teach the thematic units that the teachers had enjoyed up to that point. The plans were explicit, even giving teachers minute-to-minute timing instruction and specific language to use when teaching. Many teachers objected to this kind of district "heat" and began complaining about the use of the plans. Some principals required teachers to use them, and some principals did not. The wide variation, then, in implementation, became more and more evident.

Two key supporters of quality school-based implementation of the reading materials, the principals and the instructional coaches, continued to try to catch up with the problems of implementation. The instructional coaches were meeting regularly to study the "science of reading" but they were given limited support in how to coach teachers to quality reading instruction. As sometimes is the case, so much time was being spent on the *what* of reading that it seemed the coaching skills were being left up to each coach's innate ability. The same issue was true for building principals. "There was more of a conscious effort in building their [the principals'] reading content knowledge. There was an added push to force principals to be leaders instead of just managers. The problem became this—they were getting content knowledge but didn't have the coaching skills to work with teachers. As a result, there is great variability with principals in terms of skills to have conversations with teachers," explains Joanie Kemper, senior director of teaching and learning.

As evidenced by the long list of actions by the district, at the time of this publication (the third year of implementation of the K–2 program and the second year of the 3–5 program), there is still a sense that matters have not been completely smoothed out. "I'm still hearing from teachers that nothing's changed. I don't think teachers know what is being done to fix things," explains Diane Connelly. The perceived rigidity in the program continues to be an issue. Many teachers feel that the program doesn't allow for differences in materials or approach, and the priority plans are still being used, although the committee has been functioning to remedy the major issues in that document. Walkthroughs continue and have increased in frequency and goal. Because of a general lack of trust, the walkthroughs are viewed skeptically. Conner Austen sums it up, by articulating his perspective of the four major issues in the implementation of the work:

1. The timeliness of the decisions made by the district

2. The appropriateness of the materials and the assessments

3. The lack of thoughtful consideration of the breadth of the programs being implemented

4. The use of checklists and other means to try to "inspect" quality into the reading program

He sums up his feelings: "I really want to collaborate on this. I want all constituents to collaborate together for the benefit of students. When we are not collaborative and the decision-making is one-sided, it makes it hard on the soldiers (the teachers) because they really do care."

The leaders of the Ashton Unified School District certainly had their hands full as they led teachers into implementation of the reading program. The initiation of the program seemed so quick, preparation was not consistent from building to building, and knowledge about the program and its purpose was sketchy as teachers attempted to use it. These

(Continued)

(Continued)

initiation issues specifically affected the issues of implementation. While Masterson (2008) advocates a "ready/fire/aim" approach to change, the opinions of Ashton teachers and principals seemed to believe that there wasn't enough "ready" before the whole thing "fired." Problem after problem and perception after perception piled up and became almost insurmountable to the district leaders. Again, Joanie Kemper clearly captures the essence of the initiation and implementation hurdles: "The district is still living out the same issues they had at initiation. The initiation process worked in terms of selecting the materials; however, the initiation phase was not done well. We didn't have a clear understanding of where we wanted to go, we didn't have enough professional learning to support it, and we didn't have all the right materials to make it work. I wonder with the mistakes we made in initiation and how much of an impact those mistakes had to do with our implementation—can we recover?"

As we move into continuation, or institutionalization, and look at what leaders do to ensure that the innovation lasts, we will see how the Ashton leaders continued to resolve their issues so the program would last and have lasting positive effects on both teachers and students. We will also see what the leaders in Kingsport City Schools did and didn't do in order to ensure institutionalization of the coaching initiative.

Take a Moment

As both districts moved their changes into actual implementation, the leaders met challenges. Their willingness to honestly address the challenges and involve all stakeholders in those conversations were instrumental in maintaining the momentum of implementation. It appeared difficult for one district to overcome the implementation issues, primarily because of the way the leaders handled initiation. Reflect on actions that we know support the implementation of any change.

To what extent did the leaders of both districts

- find creative ways to message the purpose (vision of the change) so people remain focused and motivated;

- use the vision to invite open, honest conversations about the issues teachers are having when implementing the change;

- help teachers see how their day-to-day actions are purposeful and assist the district achieve the vision;

- create regular times for teachers to share their concerns about the change;

- demonstrate the leaders' understanding about their implementation concerns;

- listen more and talk less when the subject centers on the change the district was seeking;

- use the one-legged conversation technique to learn about the issues and build trust;

- find times and ways for teachers to informally share their implementation successes;

- find times for teachers to work together to troubleshoot their implementation issues or dilemmas;

- focus their conversation on their practical issues while maintaining a steady eye on the vision;

- encourage teachers to be open and honest with them regarding their implementation mindsets;

- create ways to acknowledge the short-term wins; and

- differentiate their support of teachers so they could engineer their own ways to move forward with implementation?

CHAPTER 4

ENSURING PERMANENCE

Neutralize the barriers and weave the change into the school fabric.

KEY
PRACTICE

Don't Think the Work Is Over!

Leaders who have successfully navigated the multiple implementation issues with some success may be seduced into thinking that they have done their job and that the change will continue to be implemented with great impact. Yet, "we must remember that even during full institutionalization, the work is not over because we feel we have achieved 'it'" (Tomlinson & Murphy, 2015, p. 34). Probably the biggest warning about sustaining change is this:

Even if implementation has gone really well, we are not out of the woods yet! The change will not, by itself, settle nicely into a permanent school routine without your attention, reflection, and strategic support.

After years of focused work, the move toward institutionalization signals to teachers, parents, and students that the principles and practices of the change "have been successfully woven into the fabric of the school" (Tomlinson & Murphy, 2015). Institutionalization is that phase, well into the change's maturity, when the change is entering an impactful, established age. In other words, the innovation stops being seen as something new and begins to become a part of the way the school does things. Years ago, Huberman and Miles (1984) wrote of institutionalization as the "presence of organizational conditions that signal routinization of the innovation" (p. 207). Therefore, institutionalization becomes the time when the changes are getting incorporated into the school's system of practices (Fullan, 2007). As I had said before, I think of institutionalization as when "we don't call it (the change) by name anymore." The change is simply the way we "do school."

Do Everything You Can to Secure the Change

Central to the idea of institutionalization is that the practices have become so grounded that they would even outlast the presence of the leader (Sergiovanni, 1992). Although at this point of deep implementation teachers may be experiencing a great deal of success with the change, they are still attempting to fully adapt the change into their own teaching "schemas." During this transition from implementation into institutionalization, our hope is that teachers are noticing the difference that the change is making with their students and are feeling that the incorporation of this practice into their daily practices is essential to both them and the students who inhabit their classrooms. Our job as leaders is to encourage teachers, even at this late phase, to extend the scope of what they are doing, take additional instructional risks, and "critically examine their own practices to see how these can be deepened, strengthened, and extended" (Tomlinson & Murphy, 2015, p. 34).

Institutionalization is more than just continuation. Continuation of a change might just occur because a principal or key leader simply liked the change or found it more efficient or convenient. Instead, when we are approaching institutionalization, we are looking for the structures, procedures, and organizational mindsets that are indicators that the change is being intentionally built into the school and the district (Huberman & Miles, 1984). At this point, the change is here to stay and undoing it would be dramatic and cumbersome, calling for significant organizational and classroom changes that might be detrimental to both teachers and students (Huberman & Miles, 1984).

> Central to the idea of institutionalization is that the practices have become so gounded that they would even outlast the presence of the leader.

Achieve Synchronization and "Flow"

Institutionalization signals an achievement of synchronization, "essential for excellence in execution and for energizing the corporation" (Bossidy & Charan, 2009, p. 234). During institutionalization, all of the moving parts of the organization have aligned assumptions about students, the particular educational contexts under which the students function, and what is necessary to link the independent parts of schooling and matching those parts with the goals of the school (Bossidy & Charan, 2009). When institutionalization has been reached or is about to be reached, there is a sense of "flow," which Pink (2009) describes as an experience where people "feel so utterly in control that their sense of time, place, and even self melted away" (p. 113). In "flow," there is that feeling of alignment, purpose, autonomy, mastery, and the knowledge that all of the moving parts of the organization have been adjusted to work together for the achievement of the purpose. During flow, there is more engagement than ever before, because results are being realized and personal fulfilment, while not foremost, is felt almost to the point where people are "forgetting themselves in function" (Pink, 2009, p. 113).

"Flow" is that feeling of alignment, purpose, autonomy, mastery, and the knowledge that all of the moving parts of the organization have been adjusted to work together for the achievement of the purpose.

At this point in the life of the change, there is a sense that we are facing challenges with equal parts of engagement and self-efficacy. We feel that we are achieving some degree of mastery; and although mastery requires "effort, grit, and deliberate practice" (Pink, 2009, p. 223), the pull of the change continues to attract our best efforts and deepest self-examinations. When the change has been so strategically supported and led, there is a sense that at this point of the change tenure, this innovation would be impossible to give up because of its hold on the teachers in that building.

Leadership Essential Actions During Institutionalization

Believe it or not, even if there is synchronization among the change efforts and the results, people may show some resistance to the deep adjustments they have been called to make in their practices. The same five essential leader actions that were critical during initiation and implementation are equally important during institutionalization, both to manage resistance and to ensure permanence of the change. True to our long-term change theory developed in chapter 1, the nature of these actions and how this support looks will adjust to specific needs and dilemmas that implementers face as they are attempting to make the change permanent, lasting, and impactful.

Action #1: Continue to Communicate the Purpose/Vision

During implementation, there is a uniform "attention [that is] focused on the processes and tasks of using the innovation and the best use of the information and resources. Issues of efficiency, organizing, managing, schedule, and time demands are utmost" (Hall & Hord, 2001). Because of this focus, the people trying the change may feel less certain about their ability to implement the change or the change's ability to positively impact students, leading to the implementation dip (Fullan, 2001). As we have said before, these day-to-day problems are real and may cause teachers to be in danger of losing the purpose, or the big *why* of the work.

As the change moves from implementation to institutionalization, while these issues may persist for teachers, they are probably softened by the knowledge that the change is having a positive impact on students. Although the day-to-day issues are still important, a sense of overall impact may begin to take center stage, lessening the intensity of those day-to-day issues. Even if the sense of impact begins to be powerfully felt and heard, it is still no time for the leader to stop reminding people of the purpose for their continued efforts.

Perhaps one of the most dangerous feelings during this late stage of change may be ambivalence (Zuckhoff & Gorscak, 2015). A renewed sense of purpose may help teachers continue to "untangle all of the complicated and conflicting thoughts we (they) have about the issue we're (they're) struggling with so we (they) can restore our (their) ability to think our (their) way through it" (p. 23). The focus on purpose can also help teachers continue to be at peace with the change, especially if the purpose is linked to the general positive results teachers are getting.

The lack of ambivalence contributes to a sense of confidence. During institutionalization, our hope is that teachers are facing even serious problems but feeling that they can solve them and not be consumed by self-doubt. This sense of confidence must be directly fed by school leaders. They must be in the habit, even at this late stage, of finding ways to point out when issues have been faced, teachers have dug deep into their practice, and students have been the beneficiaries of such efforts. This can be accomplished by linking the purpose to these challenges on a regular, creative, and sincere basis.

The leader's attention to challenges being met is part of her decision to periodically build in pauses, both formally and informally, to notice these issues, efforts, and successes. During the time of focused work, teachers will have felt the sense of urgency to change and act to implement the change, but without these pauses (even during institutionalization), staff members can "grow weary and frustrated with the change process and what they view as excessive work" (Hirsh, Psencik, & Brown, 2014, p. 212). Ammabile and Kramer (2011) explain that spirits are boosted and tenacity is reinforced when teachers continue to be reminded that they are making progress. Thus, the leader's function is to find times for these celebrations, either individually or in a larger group. Linking the challenges to the actions and how they have helped people get closer to their collaborative purpose also helps brace for future challenge, even at this late stage. Bolman and Deal (2008) call this helping teachers "face calamity."

Reinforce the Purpose During Institutionalization

Why Is This Action Important?	What If It Doesn't Happen?
Reinforces effort and points out how effort has been aligned to the purpose	The purpose may become "foggy" and people may not see how their efforts have helped the school achieve its goal.
Reduces ambivalence to the change	It may allow people to become neutral or feel that both their efforts to avoid the change and their efforts to embrace the change are equally undesirable.
Maintains a focus, boosts energy, and builds individual confidence	People may fall back into a fragmented way of thinking of all they are doing and lose the purpose for any of their multiple initiatives.
Prepares people to continue to face "calamity"	People may become weary of their hard work and feel that they have exhausted all of their techniques for facing continual instructional challenges.

Action #2: Continue to Listen and Be Empathetic to Concerns

As I said earlier, we usually like to focus on the positive aspects of changes in schools in an attempt to maintain energy. This is especially true when we feel that we are implementing the change with fidelity and are getting great results. Late in the change game, there will be a tendency to think that all of the major problems with implementation have been worked out. This may indeed be close to the truth. Yet, there will still be concerns that teachers have with the change. Odds are, however, that the nature of the concerns will change. If many of the concerns during implementation are about doing the work and managing its aspects, it could be that the majority of concerns during institutionalization are about results, not getting the results people anticipated, or competing demands that are making the continuation of the change difficult (Hall & Hord, 2001). The leader's task, then, is to continue to solicit and listen to these issues. If there is listening and then actions to address these unique concerns, odds are that teachers will tend to stay with the change and be more motivated to completely embed the change within their own practices.

The act of soliciting concerns, even at this late stage, is critical for the health of the change. As the critical work progresses for years and major issues are addressed and resolved, leaders may experience some "implementation fatigue" and simply seek school days when everything at school seems harmonious. This need, while entirely logical, is dangerous to the change. Even during implementation moving into institutionalization of the practice, the leader's aim is to encourage "robust dialogue," grounded in candid opinions, creativity, and critical thinking (Bossidy & Charan, 2009). Harmony, they remind us, "can be the enemy of truth. It can drive decision making underground. When harmony prevails, here's how things often get settled: after the key players leave the session, they quietly veto decisions they didn't like but didn't debate on the spot" (p. 103).

During this state of intentional sustainability, a key to soliciting concerns and honest listening is informality. As teachers are embracing the practice and seeing positive results, leaders can use informal conversations to spark questions, spontaneous problem-solving, and critical thinking (Bossidy & Charan, 2009). Leaders may want to again use the skill of one-legged conversations (Hall & Hord, 2001), that deceptively informal and efficient practice to get at the heart of the issues that are still troubling the teacher or dominating his dilemmas in implementing the change. Or, leaders may simply want to ask teachers during comfortable informal settings to "tell the story of how the change is looking in their classrooms," inviting them to process not only the operational aspects of the change but also their emotional responses and feelings—needs that they have if we are to acknowledge their efforts (Tschannen-Moran & Tschannen-Moran, 2010). In essence, the teacher stories are their "reports of the world as it is" (p. 78). By informally listening to these stories of how it is looking in their classrooms, teachers and leaders will naturally drift into conversations of hypotheses of how it might be improved.

The leader's exercise of invited dialogue, then, is an opportunity to do several things: (a) demonstrate that she is still interested in the everyday workings of the change, (b) show interest in the results teachers are getting, and (c) validate the efforts still being demonstrated by the implementers. By asking questions and inviting creative solutions to get even more results, the leader is also, in a subtle way, communicating to the teacher that this change is aiming for permanence—and while there is still work to do, the change is about to become a part of the everyday fabric of the "way we do school."

Listening to Concerns When Moving Toward Institutionalization of the Change

Why Is This Action Important?	What If It Doesn't Happen?
Continues an empathetic partnership between the leader and teachers	People may still have concerns about the change at this phase; if they don't have that partnership with principals, they may feel their concerns are now not valid.
Reinforces the efforts people are making to achieve results with their students	People may feel that their efforts are "not good enough" and harshly judge their own competence.
Gives leaders and teachers an informal forum for problem-solving, creativity, and troubleshooting	People may feel that they have gone "deep enough" with implementation and not pursue even more sophisticated practice.

Action #3: Provide Pathways for People to Work Together to Support Mutual Effectiveness

During the processes of institutionalization, the most valuable professional learning will occur at schools and will focus on more sophisticated ways to determine implementation excellence and results. While training was possibly a good professional learning vehicle during initiation, more job-embedded, school-based problem-solving experiences were valuable during implementation. As we move into institutionalization, the creation of informal networks will bring minds together, allowing them to "deisolate themselves and put aside day-to-day distractions to focus on the strategies and skills necessary to lead to high achievement" (Hirsh et al., 2014, p. 196).

These networks need not look complicated or formal—in fact, the savvy leader will differentiate these networks of implementers based on timing and the teachers' needs, interests, and issues. Looking internally to pool the collective intelligence of the implementing teachers is a wise choice. Leaders, then, must still create these opportunities within the daily schedules for teachers to talk about their practices and model for them how to go deep into their own self-examinations to determine effectiveness. This regular, school-based guided time will promote the interdependence (Little, 2008) that invites teachers to move away from simply talking about problem-solving and provides the time for them to "bring stories of the classroom into group meetings and to convey them with enough specificity and transparency that people can have meaningful conversations about them. These teachers share a curriculum,

Leaders, then, must still create these opportunities within the daily schedules for teachers to talk about their practices and model for them how to go deep into their own self-examinations to determine effectiveness.

they share an understanding of particular instructional approaches, and they're able to have conversations that are really anchored in their shared understanding of each other's teaching" (p. 55).

When moving from implementation to institutionalization, the job-embedded professional support is focused on not only teaching using the new practices but the degree to which learning occurs with students. As networks of teachers consult with and coach each other, leaders hope that the conversations are moving away from simple problem-solving and toward "cooperative, inquiry-based work" (Hawley & Valli, 1999). The following professional learning designs (Croft, Coggshall, Dolan, & Powers, 2010) are grounded in these networks of informal examinations of skill and results, and any of them could be quite significant in moving the change forward into more permanence:

- Teachers work together to write lesson plans to target a difficult instructional concept or one that has proven difficult to teach in the past.
- Teachers teach a concept, then collect samples of student work and collaboratively analyze them, using a tuning protocol to solicit joint analysis and dialogue.
- Teachers engage in case discussions to critically analyze teaching when they are not in the act itself, using video, multimedia, and so on.
- Teachers meet and analyze each other's work such as lesson plans, assessments, student work, and more.
- Teachers coach each other through an instructional segment.
- Teachers engage in professional learning communities where they collaborate to analyze their practice and discuss new strategies and tactics, testing them in the classroom and reporting the results to each other.

Any of these job-embedded designs could promote the continuation of dialogue and self-examination that is needed during institutionalization. As said before, leaders may not want to "prescribe" the design for certain groups of teacher networks; instead, they may want the teachers to meet, discuss their goals for working together, and then ask them to select the design that best meets their needs, level of trust, and working culture.

Creating Pathways for People to Support Their Mutual Effectiveness

Why Is This Action Important?	What If It Doesn't Happen?
Focuses on the actual work and the "doing" of the change	People may feel that the issues still remaining are not acknowledged or appreciated.
Acknowledges that informal, job-embedded designs best support teachers when they are doing the work	Without an intentional focus on interdependence, teachers may feel isolated and may lose focus or effort.
Connects teachers with each other as informal resources	It stifles the continuous need for reflection and resource dissemination.

Action #4: Build Their Trust in You, the Work, and Each Other

As we have said before, any lasting change in schools will be accomplished by individuals; as these individuals explore the new change and implement it in their classrooms, they will want to express their ideas and seek their voice to explore the practices more deeply (Brown, 2017). During implementation, teachers are seeking to adapt, not adopt, the change into their practices. Each individual will have different challenges and successes and will want to seek dialogue about the change with both the leader and their colleagues. When moving toward institutionalization, those same individuals will not only continue to pay attention to their execution of the work but also want to reflect on the work, collaborate with others, and work to make the practice even more useful.

Trust will continue to be built in leaders, the work, and each other by allowing and encouraging this reflection and transparent dialogue about the change. In fact, as teachers are more and more involved in the implementation of the work, their concerns will naturally shift from "how do you do it easily?" to "what is the impact, how are others doing it, and how can we even make it better?" Hall and Hord (2001) call these kinds of concerns "impact concerns" and imply that even during late stages of implementation and institutionalization, after years of work, the implementers will still continue to have emotional reactions and concerns to their work around the change. There are essentially three kinds of concerns that teachers during institutionalization may begin to direct toward leaders. "Consequence concerns deal with increasing effectiveness and impact in one's own classroom; collaboration concerns focus on working with one or more colleagues (to make the change more useful); and refocusing concerns indicate that the person has ideas about a possibly more effective alternative" (p. 62). No matter which type of concern is apparent, most of those worries will be focused at this stage on improving the impact of the change on students, because the mechanics of the change have generally been worked out (Hall & Hord, 2001).

Again, trust is built by soliciting these concerns and engaging in informal dialogue around them. These informal conversations will tend to narrow or collapse the "us versus them" mentality that sometimes pervades a large-scale change, bringing together people in different roles in schools to focus on understanding how the change is getting them closer to their purpose. In addition, trust will continue to be built in the work of the change by encouraging the continuation of conversation about the change and refusing to think that the change is "done."

At this point, an important trust-building strategy is a process that Paul Zak (2017) calls "ovation." He defines ovation as "recognizing colleagues who contribute to the organization's success. Ovation explains 67 percent of organizational trust" (p. 31). Ovation is not a group of simple celebrations that may focus on general, nonspecific contributions. Ovation is the leader's act of creating moments where the recognition is unexpected, tangible, and personal (Zak, 2017). It is time sensitive in that it occurs promptly; it is change sensitive in that it discovers and publicly describes the practices that led the organization toward its purpose; and it is personal in that it is directly related to the individual who tested out the practice and achieved something. This kind of recognition of effort and achievement is akin to the kinds of celebrations that Hirsh et al. (2014) encourage when they suggest that these celebrations need to be authentic and not just come from the traditionally recognized leader of the school.

Building Trust During Implementation

Why Is This Action Important?	What If It Doesn't Happen?
Facilitates honest conversations about the results of their work and their continued issues, building confidence in continuing the work and reaching even more powerful results	People may feel that they shouldn't have issues at this stage; the invitation to talk about them will increase involvement and maintain their motivation.
Creates opportunities to listen to issues causing dissatisfaction so the change will not be betrayed and will provide a pathway for discontent and perhaps solution finding	People may share their concerns covertly or create dissatisfaction among their peers.
Creates times for collegial ovations to encourage idea sharing, problem-solving, and deepening trust in the work and in each other	People may not feel that they are being noticed for their long-term efforts and begin to move away from deep implementation of the change.

Action #5: Facilitate a Sense of Accomplishment

During implementation, leaders will want to continue to find ways teachers can experience short-term wins. That sense of accomplishment, although small, will help to maintain a sense of mastery, motivating teachers to continue to work toward larger accomplishments (Pink, 2009). As the change progresses through implementation and into institutionalization, leaders will want to continue to find ways to celebrate the short-term wins and risks that teachers took to achieve even better results. Also during this time, leaders will want to encourage the informal professional learning networks so teachers can consider "how did my planned solutions (to the implementation issues) work?" (Zuckoff & Gorscak, 2015).

The sense of accomplishment for implementers evolves from short term to a reflection on the trials and errors of deep implementation. The accomplishment comes from both successes and failures—if the solution worked well, it is a time to stay with those solutions; if the solution did not produce the desired result, then institutionalization is the time to consider new points of view about the issue. Through the leader's informal networking and listening sessions, teachers will explore those continuing issues and, with the trust they now have in the work, they will be propelled into attempting new means of overcoming those hurdles.

Remembering that teachers often have a need to collaborate and create an even more powerful version of the change during institutionalization helps us realize the other kinds of accomplishments they may feel during institutionalization. While their work has primarily been focused on their individual implementation of the change, institutionalization invites this network-rich set of conversations about the system that is supporting the change. Individuals, then, will get a sense of accomplishment and involvement by talking openly and honestly about the issues that could weaken the change (Bossidy & Charan, 2009), such as the following:

- How strong is the capacity of our school to continue to execute this change?
- Is our plan still sharply focused?
- Is this still the right change to make?
- Are other, newer changes competing with this one?
- Is the purpose still clear?

Facilitate a Sense of Accomplishment During Institutionalization

Why Is This Action Important?	What If It Doesn't Happen?
Invites people to take an active part in the overall reflection on results and improvements	Teachers may just focus on their own implementation issues in their classrooms and not share an organizational loyalty to the purpose.
Allows for individual teachers to continue to feel a part of a larger community, achieving the purpose	It fragments the work and the message.
Continues to stress short-term wins and an equal emphasis on achieving results	People may not feel that they can invest what they should unless they are still experiencing day-to-day wins.

Take a Moment

It is challenging to handle the issues of long-term implementation and make the transition to institutionalization of the practices. Consider these questions.

To what extent do I

- give people a real chance to work through their nagging implementation issues;

- notice the effort people are making to incorporate the change into their own practices;

- find time for personal, meaningful celebrations;

- continue to ask teachers for the concerns they have about the change;

- network teachers to continue to problem solve and rely on each other to deepen and sustain their new practices;

- regularly create school-based, job-embedded informal ways for teachers to keep learning about the change and how to implement it;

- build trust with teachers and me around the work;

- demonstrate my knowledge of the change practice to promote trust in the work;

- help people focus on the purpose of the change as they are experiencing success; and

- work to keep competing initiatives from weakening the change?

OUR TWO SCHOOL DISTRICTS AND THE ATTEMPTS TO INSTITUTIONALIZE THE WORK

In reviewing how both sets of district leaders implemented their initiatives, you can see that there were some successes and some actions that resulted in a range of reactions, from confusion to downright resistance and upheaval. The Kingsport City Schools initiative was begun in the summer of 2016; the Ashton Unified reading instructional initiative was also started that same year. You will see that, at the time of this publication, both are at really different places in the lives of their initiatives.

Kingsport City Schools

The Kingsport City Schools leaders wanted a new coaching model that still provided the support principals were uniformly requesting. The director of schools and district leaders initiated a more balanced, positive coaching model that simultaneously supported effective curriculum understanding as well as instructional practices that would be invaluable to the principals of their 11 schools. Initiation and implementation of the coaching change appeared to go rather smoothly. The coaches and principals were asked to create and adhere to a "coaching contract" that would guide their work together at their particular schools. The titles of the coaches were changed to indicate this new coaching initiative had little to do with the old coaching model. Coaches, now called InDeS (instructional design specialists), were encouraged to build relationships and form working partnerships with not only teachers in need but also teachers who were already achieving great results. Multiple sources of data were collected to show how coaching was proceeding and what kinds of things teachers were asking for help. Principals participated in parallel professional learning to ascertain how they needed to function to make results at their schools more predictable and stable. I led quarterly professional learning sessions with InDeS to keep up with their skills and to problem solve.

As of early 2020, the coaching initiative was in its fourth full year of work. School achievement results have been positive and encouraging. In the school year 2018–2019, 6 of the 11 schools were recognized by the state as having the highest achievement quotient when demographics, economic diversity, and student performance metrics are used (the highest number in the district's history). The coaches continue to meet on a monthly basis. Principals are consistently utilizing the coaches in impactful ways and verbalize the importance of the coaches in their schools.

(Continued)

(Continued)

The culture of each school appears to have embraced their InDeS with eager arms. There is virtually no conversation among teachers or leaders about "the way we used to do coaching." Let's see what district leaders did at the beginning of institutionalization. An examination of these actions produced both challenges to the initiative and efforts toward permanence.

Build Trust and Listen to Concerns

1. The position of the director of professional development, who supervised the work of the coaches and served as a liaison between schools and the coaches, was eliminated in the 2019–2020 budget. Coaches were not assigned to another person; instead, coaches began to meet on a monthly basis with the elementary and secondary directors as well as the assistant director of schools to ensure communication and continuity.

Provide Ongoing Learning

2. Coaches were asked to take a "deep dive" into coaching, particularly for math and literacy achievement. They participated in professional learning that was designed for just that, and they were encouraged to combine these subject coaching skills with the general skills they learned during the first few years of coaching implementation.

Sense of Accomplishment

3. Coaches met with the math and literacy specialists on a continual basis to put into practice some of the techniques and strategies they learned at the math and literacy coaching professional learning. They worked collaboratively with the math and literacy specialists to set short-term goals and to monitor the results of their work in schools.

Sense of Accomplishment

4. District leaders are now working with the coaches to design a comprehensive way to assess the coaching initiative, now that they feel student results should be a key source of data. This model will continue to be used as the district clearly establishes institutionalization of coaching in all schools.

Clarity of Messaging

5. Organizational dilemmas and operational challenges are openly discussed among the directors and coaches to remain true to the model. These challenges include (a) the recent departure of one of the high school coaches without a replacement named; (b) the elimination of the professional learning director position, a person who supervised the coaches; (c) school leadership changes; (d) new initiatives that might compete with the coaching initiative for funding and priority; and (e) confusion about the differences between coaching and a "teacher leader" model just implemented.

In Kingsport City Schools, there were challenges that threatened to slow the progression of implementation to institutionalism or weaken the coaching program altogether. The coaches' direct supervisor and mentor, the professional learning director, began a new position as a result of restructuring. The fact that principals had a cursory understanding of the coaches' roles proved to be a challenge at the beginning of implementation. So, instead of letting the coaching role "drift" toward something unintentional, the principals were engaged in ongoing training and dialogue about coaching roles and successes. Yet, principal understanding of the purpose of coaching continued to be an issue of concern well into implementation and beginning institutionalization.

The coaches experienced some issues as well. They had high levels of energy and were eager to help in profound ways. There was a general feeling of impatience among them when some initial constraints were put on them. While the coaches began to sense the early fruits of their labor, they were asked to keep voluminous amounts of data regarding their duties, which was overwhelming at times.

During full implementation, it became apparent that most school principals were not directly connecting the work of the coaches to their school improvement plans. As a result, district leaders determined that there was not the desired clarity of the improvement work at each school. During the second year of InDeS implementation, they asked principals to focus on school vision statements and the incorporation of the coaching support into their yearly "change plans" to accomplish their visions.

As we have said before, at the date of publication, the Kingsport coaching program is in its fourth year of implementation. One of the signals for implementation moving into institutionalization is that "we don't call it anything anymore." This is apparently true of the coaching initiative in Kingsport City Schools because the people working there do not call it a "change" or "something new we are working on." The Kingsport leaders did not succeed because they avoided common issues; rather, they have probably succeeded because they were eager to learn of the issues and were committed to addressing them. Even at the mature time of the coaching work, the leaders have made sure that the huge foundational concepts of the coaching change continue. Funding for the coaches has not waivered, principals are now describing how valuable the coaches are to their work, and student achievement is on the rise. Systems to continue to evaluate the initiative are being designed to show lasting impact. The new director, who came from a similar district in Tennessee, chose not to change the coaching model and continues to support it with funding, mentoring, and supervision.

(Continued)

(Continued)

The InDeS continue to meet as much as they did during their first three years and are continuing to participate in professional learning. While these ideas add to the stability of the change, there are still worries. "We have to keep paying attention to professional learning and onboarding of new InDeS will always be an issue that must be dealt with. Someone needs to step up as their advocate and make sure the work is getting done," Stephanie Potter reminds us.

The successes and the attention to the issues are both positive signs that the district is thinking of the coaching model as an integral part of the schooling structures. As we have said in this chapter, however, there will be challenges. "This is a critical year [2019–2020] for the program to make sure it stays pure, more sophisticated, and that it lasts," comments Brian Cinnamon, the secondary director. Cinnamon is most concerned that the initiative doesn't "shift the InDeS duties to other responsibilities that might not matter as much."

Cinnamon's comments echo what seems to be a cautiously positive approach to institutionalizing the initiative. While the results have been overwhelmingly positive, there is still a desire among district leaders to make sure the initiative's purpose doesn't "become foggy" over time or gradually drift into functions that are suspect.

Concerns about competing initiatives or confusing initiatives also dominate district leaders' thoughts. "There is still confusion over the difference between the InDeS functions and the functions of the teacher leaders. People still don't know the difference and are asking for clarification," explains Potter. In late 2019, Cinnamon described a new concept, the "portrait of the graduate," which the director asked all schools to address. While Cinnamon was easily able to describe the value of the new initiative, he was not sure about the linkage between the portrait of the graduate process and the school visioning process. He believes that because the InDeS have been so involved in school visioning, it will be imperative to connect the portrait of the graduate to the school vision work. He explains: "The portrait of the graduate has been a bit confusing, frankly. I know it is a good thing, but will it change the work of the InDeS? One of the things that has come up from the portrait work is that it seems out of sequence with the visioning work. Will the work of the InDeS, the work of school improvement, and the portrait work be merged? Or will the work of the InDeS be the loser?"

Tackling competing demands and aligning them continues, then, to be a challenge, even in Kingsport City Schools, a district that enjoys a reputation for being innovative. Ashley Carter, one of the original InDeS, summarizes her perspective: "We need to be sensitive about the institutionalization of the InDeS or it could fall away if we don't have a continual vision for the position and a plan moving forward." She believes that now, the quality of instructional conversations between the principal and the InDeS is one of the most impactful things in schools. She is passionate about the coaching initiative and hopeful about its continuation, and lists six "things" that must still be present (from her perspective) if the initiative is to have lasting institutionalization and impact:

- Continue to have a clear vision for the InDeS and a plan to use them

- Cultivate the internal leadership of the InDeS

- Keep having conversations with principals about powerful ways to use the InDeS to prevent role "drift"

- Make sure the InDeS have a direct role in school improvement

- Keep the contracts between InDeS and renegotiate them each year

- Have periodic meetings within the district among all InDeS and principals to promote conversation and problem solving

The Ashton Unified School District

Although the Ashton Unified School District also began their K–5 reading initiative during the summer of 2016, the district did not experience the same consistent implementation success that the Kingsport City Schools leaders enjoyed. Remember that the decision to implement a new reading program in grades K–5 in the Ashton Unified School District was led by two groups: (a) the district's school board members who were alarmed at the consistently mediocre student performance and (b) the new superintendent and her curriculum and instruction staff. There was a sense of urgency in this decision for a change. The new program and materials were purchased and district leaders planned for the implementation of the program in grades K–2 only during the first year, with grades 3–5 brought on in the next school year. Even though the teachers had participated in voluntary summer training regarding the reading program and a mandated reading "in-service day" as school started, all of the materials were not at buildings for early viewing and planning by the teachers. For many teachers at many of the elementary buildings, the first time they saw the reading materials was on the first day of school with their students. The district leaders quickly recognized

(Continued)

(Continued)

their implementation problems, and yet their attempts to provide more structure and support often resulted in more frustration. Implementation moved along, albeit slow and inconsistent from school to school.

Institutionalization is the transition from implementation problem solving to decisions to make the change permanent and impactful. For Ashton, most of the major problems that appeared during initiation and implementation continued to exist going into the fourth year of effort. Some of the decisions district leaders made actually exacerbated the implementation problems. Let's review the major implementation issues that plagued the district from the start:

- Uneven teacher use of the materials and a lack of knowledge about the use of the materials

- Principal preparation, understanding, and support of implementation at the schools

- The lack of professional learning (training) or the inconsistent quality of training at first to prepare teachers

- Instructional coaches' confusion about the implementation of the reading initiative and their roles in it

- A struggle between the prescribed priority plans and teacher flexibility in choosing materials and strategies for their particular students

- A sense that many teachers had that the district was "doing nothing to help the problems"

A comprehensive teacher survey had been given in the spring of 2019, and the summary of those survey results revealed that the most intense reading program issues appeared to be the rigidity of the priority plans, which were district-created pacing guides to show teachers how to incorporate all the parts of quality reading into their schedules. Teachers felt that these plans were so prescribed and structured that they allowed for no variation depending on the ability and pre-reading experiences of their students. Some of the teachers' concerns appeared to be valid. In fact, the priority plans *did* mandate the use of certain materials and even went so far as to plan out the teacher's instruction minute by minute.

The other intense concern from the teacher survey was the kind and amount of support they felt they were getting from their building and district leadership. Instructional coaches were in their rooms to observe reading instruction, but many teachers felt these visits were punitive because their individual reading instructional skills were being shared with principals. Principal support for the change was, at best, uneven. In some schools, principals felt that they must support the priority plans and mandated the use of them; in other schools, principals told teachers that they didn't have to use the plans or the materials in the program. Teachers complained that they had been inadequately prepared to use the materials, since the only training they received was one day of training, delivered by their instructional coach, at their buildings.

These issues indicated that, even after years of implementation efforts, the district was still in the throes of an implementation dip (see chapter 1). That dip was classically evident in the decreased enthusiasm for the reading initiative and the constant vocalization of the same issues. District leaders quickly recognized many of the implementation problems and realized that the chronic issues were so powerful that they threatened the implementation altogether. Although they had hoped that the beginning of the fourth year would signal the transition from implementation to institutitonalization, they found themselves instead responding to the same implementation issues they had heard for years. These district actions were put into place to address the issues, with their intent noted:

1. District leaders compiled the results of the teacher survey (spring, 2019) and shared a thorough executive summary with all K–5 teachers in the summer and fall of 2019, the beginning of that school year. In addition, the district leadership and the local union drafted a joint letter to all involved teachers, sharing what they had learned and, in general, the actions that would be taken.

    Clarity of Messaging and Sense of Accomplishment

2. A teacher task force organized and began meeting. Their task was to review the district vision for reading and then make both formatting and content changes and improvements to the priority plans.

    Listening to Concerns and Build Trust

3. The priority plan task force published a document explaining the reason for the reading program and the priority plans, complete with a list of "negotiables" and "non-negotiables." This document was distributed to all teachers and principals in late January of 2020.

    Clarity of Messaging and Purpose of the Change

4. I worked with district leaders to create a 2019–2020 program assessment plan, using multiple data sources and multiple points of collection. The intent of the plan was to get a clearer sense of how it was going three times a year and share those results with teachers and use for program adjustments.

    Sense of Accomplishment

(Continued)

(Continued)

It is notable to review what the district did not do as a result of their implementation issues. They did not appear to directly and carefully align the coaches' responsibilities and assist them in acquiring (a) the reading knowledge they needed to support teachers better and (b) the coaching skills that would build trust between the coach and the teacher. The district did find time to work with principals as leaders of reading during their regular principals' meetings. While this seemed like a good idea, it didn't appear to reach the goal of creating consistently effective leaders of reading and effective partners with their teachers in reading improvement. As a result, instead of working more diligently to create this reading partnership, they secured another consultant to work with principals on coaching and feedback skills. Principals did not uniformly see the connection between that coaching skills work and the reading work; instead, they looked at the new consulting work as being "more work" and not necessarily connected to the goal of having powerful conversations with teachers about reading.

Contributing to the ongoing unrest was a shift in upper-level district leadership. In 2019, a new internal candidate was appointed head of the elementary principals. This new staff member's behavior indicated that he might either (a) not be fully buying into the collaborative partnership district leaders had struck with the local union or (b) not be fully cognizant of the purpose of the reading change or the issues that had already arisen. "We were getting the distinct feeling that [name] was not listening, and that [name] feels his way is the right way and there is no conversation about it," one interviewee (name withheld) stated. While this issue contributed to the overall feeling of futility, the dominant undercurrent for teachers continued to be the sense that "nothing is changing" for us to make it (the reading implementation) better. "I know [the institutionalization of a reading initiative] is a long process and all of the things we are trying are good, but I'm still hearing that nothing's changed," Diane Connelly explains. She commented that she is aware of the things that are changing, but "out there," there is still a feeling that implementation structures are too rigid and that they are not feeling the improvements in their daily practices.

Joanie Kemper, in her district curriculum leadership role, is positive but realistic on the possible success of the initiative. She feels that she and her colleagues are still scrambling to correct the weaknesses in initiation and implementation. "We are trying hard to recover from this K–5 thing; the problem is, we will be going through another K–5 reading curriculum review in a couple of years (as mandated by local policy, the curriculum review recommends any materials changes every five years). Will we still be trying to recover from this as we launch into another reading curriculum review?"

In spite of the overwhelming troubles, the Ashton school leaders worked hard to address the issues. Their creation of a program assessment plan that looked at multiple measures of program success, including teacher interviews, in-classroom observations for program consistency, focus groups with instructional coaches, and student performance data, was really needed to give leaders and implementers a sense of overall district accomplishment. There was dismay, however, when some of those data were gathered. During fall of 2019 "implementation snapshots," informal, non-evaluative classroom walkthroughs to look at consistency of program components, were conducted and the overall results were disheartening. Continuing to meet with a K–5 program implementation committee to openly discuss the issues was a key action to continue to build trust. The teacher task force, formed to examine priority plan changes and format adjustments, illustrated another transparent means of addressing these plans, which ranked at the top of teacher complaints in the spring 2019 teacher survey.

The lack of trust that permeates the Ashton implementation dialogue still appears to hound the district. There is a feeling among some district leaders that the union's involvement in the program implementation dialogue is suspect. "I believe the union used this program implementation as a leverage point in their contract negotiations," explains Debra Olson. "They manufactured some of the issues to make them look worse than they were." Even though the district continued the K–5 program implementation team, the group's makeup was particularly fragile. The union selected some of the members and the district selected some. The lack of trust among them and with district leaders who were facilitating the meetings was readily apparent. During some of the testy meetings, some members walked out and refused to join the group for the rest of the meeting. Body language and "parking lot" conversations surfaced issues that, because they were not addressed, continued to infect the workings of the team. Many district officials participated in the collaborative makeup of the team although they were not sure the team knew what to do about the issues. Debra Olson was particularly clear on her remedies to the issues. During our interview, she easily communicated her solutions but wasn't quite confident that the district leadership groups and the implementation team would arrive at the same conclusions. Her ideas to pull the district out of its nagging implementation dip included these:

- One early release day per week for buildings to learn more about the competencies of teaching reading

(Continued)

(Continued)

- Targeted professional learning for teachers on formative assessment, understanding reading data, and reading standards

- A requirement for each elementary school to build a plan to show how they were going to work to achieve greater reading achievement

- Principal facilitation of professional learning communities at schools

- Targeted differentiated district support of each school, depending on "where the school is" in reading excellence

At the time of this publication, the Ashton implementation continues to progress along a rocky path. The Ashton story is a good one, because it points out that time alone will not move the change forward into institutionalization. It is also a useful story to point out the realization that implementation will suffer if initiation is not strategic and thoughtful. Even though the district was entering the fourth year of implementation of the K–2 reading program and hopes were that by this time the change should be nearing permanence, the district's issues in that fourth year almost exactly echoed the problems that plagued the district during the first and second years. While there were pockets of great reading improvement and achievement across those grades, the progress was not consistently positive and the results still varied widely from school to school. Struggles still abounded. Wounds had not healed from the injuries sustained during initiation.

Both of our districts have worked hard in their efforts to implement their changes. Both of our districts are focused on change permanence. My conversations with all of the interviewees from both districts were insightful. When I talked to my Ashton interviewees, it was interesting that they didn't really talk about permanence at all. It was simply not on their horizons because they were still in the throes of trying to solve their implementation issues and move past teacher perceptions that the district really was not to be trusted to effectively roll out a new venture.

In contrast, the Kingsport City Schools interviewees focused much of our conversations on making sure that the InDeS, the coaching program in all schools, lasted. They believed that they were experiencing what Huberman and Miles (1984) called "stable use." In stable change management, there is "an explicit systemwide commitment to continued use of the innovation, as well as provisions to stabilize that use" (p. 221).

They summarize the possibility of institutionalization of the change as hinging on these six elements (1984):

- Administrative pressure to implement the program

- No serious or lasting resistance

- A reasonable amount of teacher-administrator harmony

- Few "assistance gaps"

- A large percentage of trained users

- Stability of program leaders

In institutionalization of a major change, the culture of teaching and learning changes. In essence, implementation alters people's actions and new behavior is seen to produce benefit for a period of time. Implementation transitions into institutionalization as people feel and see the connection between their new actions and performance improvement (Kotter, 2012). This shift in the norms and values "occurs mostly in the very last stage of the process, or at least the very last stage in each cycle of the process" (Kotter, 2012, p. 165). As Kotter (2012) reminds us, "Only at the end of the change cycle do most of [the behavioral changes] become anchored in the culture" (p. 165).

Both districts wanted to begin institutionalizing their changes, and yet one district continued to face implementation challenges, which made it difficult to move toward permanence. The other district seems to be nearing institutionalization, as (a) the change is not really referred to anymore as something new and (b) the district is enjoying substantial achievement partially as a result of the change. The progress from implementation to institutionalization is still challenging, even for leaders of districts who are enjoying success with their change. Permanence is not easily achieved.

Take a Moment

Consider these questions. To what extent did the district leaders

- give people a real chance to work through their nagging implementation issues;

(Continued)

(Continued)

- notice the effort people are making to incorporate the change into their own practices;

- find time for personal, meaningful celebrations regarding the change;

- continue to ask teachers for the concerns they have about the change;

- network teachers to continue to problem solve and rely on each other to deepen and sustain their new practices;

- regularly create school-based, job-embedded informal ways for teachers to keep learning about the change and how to implement it;

- build trust with teachers and leaders around the work;

- demonstrate leaders' knowledge of the change practice to promote trust in the work;

- help people focus on the purpose of the change as they were experiencing success; and

- work to keep competing initiatives from weakening the change?

CHAPTER 5

ANTICIPATING SOME PUSHBACK

Understand the nature of resistance and then act accordingly.

Accept and Appreciate That Resistance Will Happen at Some Point in the Change

Some time ago, I was an eager elementary principal and was looking for a change in schools. My superintendent knew that I was ambitious and wanted varieties of leadership experiences, so he offered me an elementary principalship in a particularly challenging school. I was going to follow a principal who was (and still is) one of my good friends, and her

style of leadership was wildly different from mine. Study the following
story of what happened to spark resistance from one of the teachers
with whom I was about to work.

My principal friend had been frustrated with the lack of student
achievement growth in her tenure, and just before she left that
school (that I was about to lead), she made some teacher grade-
level changes and informed those teachers of the changes before
she turned the reins over to me.

Teresa was one of those teachers who was moved to a different
grade because she had not been productive in the fourth grade, a
grade she had taught for several years. My principal friend moved
her to sixth grade, a non-tested grade. I think the principal's
theory was that Teresa might indeed relate more to students of
that age, that she was capable of learning the curriculum; and to
be honest, I believe she wanted her removed from a tested grade
level to minimize her unproductive state testing results.

These kinds of elementary grade level moves usually occur at
the end of the school year and are based on a rather thin theory
that moving teachers to new grade levels offers them a chance to
start all over again. I have some pretty strong feelings about the
efficacy of moving non-voluntary teachers to different grades to
"shake things up" or to raise achievement scores. Yet, on many
occasions, this is the principal's way of pushing for change.

Teresa was rather furious when she was informed of the change.
Not known for building strong adult or student relationships, she
was unsettled by the move to the sixth-grade teaching position.
I was the new principal, and before that first school year of my
leadership began, she asked me to move her back to fourth
grade. I had already decided to honor the previous principal's
moves, so I respectfully refused Teresa's request and explained
that this had been the previous principal's decision based on
her analysis of what needed to happen. Several days after that
conversation, I had phone calls from Teresa's husband, demanding
that I move her back to fourth grade. Teresa persisted in her
request until the year started, and I began to think that this might
be a long year for her and me.

I was right. Teresa resisted participating in all of our work that year;
she refused to take any leadership roles in her grade-level team,
and she found all sorts of problems to "share with me," which
caused me unmeasurable fatigue and aggravation. Our working
relationship continued to skid; my classroom visits to Teresa's

classroom uncovered some significant curriculum and instruction issues, and our feedback conversations were strained. She refused to engage with me about her work and change in any way. Teresa was overtly resistant to everything we tried to accomplish at the school. She wasn't even willing to passively ride out the changes we attempted to implement; instead, she openly worked against them and attempted to rally support for the opposition with her colleagues. I have to admit that I was irritated by her lack of energy and focus. It's difficult for me to say, but I also found it hard to care about the personal side of Teresa—why didn't she see the urgency of working better for the students at the school?

I was promoted four years into the principalship of that school, and can honestly say that my work with Teresa never improved much during our time together at that school. Years of experience and age has allowed me to see Teresa's issues more clearly, however. It was predictable that Teresa would be upset with the grade-level change as it threw her into a new world of collegial relationships, more mature students, and curriculum she may not have clearly understood. She was confronted by a principal (me) who was focused on improving student achievement at the school and impatient with those who didn't share his focus. My unwillingness to listen to Teresa's issues because I didn't value them, along with my unwillingness to build some kind of personal relationship with her, reinforced her perception that I didn't think she was worthy of either.

Now, let's think about our journey together. So far, we have been reflecting on change, the phases of change, and five critical leadership behaviors that are essential for leading change that is designed to last. We have seen how two vastly different school districts addressed the phases of change as they promoted a major improvement in their districts. Our premise has been that if leaders thoughtfully acknowledge the life span of their change and where they are in it, and if they combine that with a willingness to adjust their actions to support continuous growth, resistance to change will be reduced. If people experience this kind of relationship-rich, results-focused behavior from their leaders, they will be more motivated to stay with the change until it becomes deep, impactful, and permanent.

Teresa's story is not that unusual, and all of us have numerous stories of resistance that we encountered as we led change. Even though the resisters are usually few in number, the issues of resistance can completely confound us. Of all the topics that I'm asked to address in my school leader coaching and consulting, resistance is probably the most requested one. Resistance makes us mad, confuses us, makes us question

> Resistance makes us mad, confuses us, makes us question our own abilities, and can whittle away at an initiative.

our own abilities, and can whittle away at an initiative. Even though we have addressed resistance in every chapter to this point—weaving together "where you are in the change" with significant actions designed to perpetuate and stabilize the change—the examples of "Teresas in our lives" makes me think that a separate chapter on this difficult topic is necessary. This additional time spent on resistance will allow us to fully explore the nature of the behavior and why it may happen.

Realize the Complexities of Resistance and Why It Triggers Strong Emotions in Us

A synthesis of the Merriam-Webster online dictionary definitions of resistance is this: "opposition, retarding, or a psychological defense mechanism wherein a patient [person] rejects, denies, or otherwise opposes efforts by another to help." Essentially, resistance to me is anything from an overt to a subtle rejection of an idea or change. Resistance can be easily witnessed in the words and actions of an individual, or it can reside quietly within a person's behavior and be hardly noticed by anyone. We often think of resistance as the former—an "in your face" hard rejection of the proposed way of doing things. And yet, resistance seems to function along a range of behaviors—all the way from the hard, noticeable, vocal rejection to the habitual reluctance of an individual to embrace new developments.

I have rarely met a school leader who relishes all of the resistance he feels and hears in his school. Often, we just don't understand the nature of or the trigger for the resistance. We have an emotional reaction to the resistance and feel that the resistance is a personal confrontation to our efforts. We simply don't like it and it confuses us with its lack of logic (from our perspective). "We see someone trapped in a behavior that's causing pain for themselves and everyone around them, and we think, why can't they just see what they're doing and stop it?" (Bechtle, 2012, p. 121).

As confounding as resistance is to us, we can't lead thinking that every one of our changes we champion will be met with people who wish the change would go away. Lawrence (1969) warns us about this cynical view of human behavior and the perception that resistance will *always* happen. "The process is clear—whenever people (who are supposed to buy the new ideas) are treated as if they were bullheaded, the way they are used to being treated changes; and they will be bullheaded in resisting that change." If we make the mistake of suspecting that all of our great changes will be met with considerable resistance, we will be lured into believing that our job is to "overcome resistance." Rick DuFour, a longtime friend of mine, once told me, "The moment I think I need to overcome the resistance I'm seeing, I know I'm in trouble. There might be something to be learned from it." Again, Lawrence reinforced this idea when he suggests that resistance might be best thought of as a useful red flag—a signal that something is going wrong (1969). Unfortunately, he reminds us that the resistance may tell us that something is going wrong, but it won't tell us what is wrong. Therefore, when resistance appears, it is time to listen so we can learn from the problem and figure out where the trouble lies (Lawrence, 1969).

Know the Catalysts for Resistance

Resistance usually happens for a reason. Powell and Kusuma-Powell (2015) remind us that as adults face challenges in their own professional success, they are often met with either technical challenges or adaptive challenges (p. 65). Lawrence (1969) agrees with these two challenges, although he refers to the adaptive challenge as a social challenge. These two kinds of challenges may be felt by any individuals anywhere along the life span of the change—initiation, implementation, or institutionalization—and can trigger resistance against the work. Leaders benefit from knowing the definitions of each.

A *technical challenge* to the work is when the person is being asked to make a "measurable modification in the physical routines of the job" (Lawrence, 1969, p. 4). Technical challenges require the person to acquire information and address the change with this information. The idea here is that the new information will somehow help the person alter his or her behavior and capabilities (Powell & Kusuma-Powell, 2015). An example of a technical challenge is when a teacher is asked to use a new software package that she doesn't yet know how to use.

An *adaptive or social challenge* to the work is when the person is asked to make the change but suspects that the change will alter his or her established relationships in the organization (Lawrence, 1969) or require him or her to rethink his or her deeply held values, beliefs, assumptions, or even professional identity (Powell & Kusuma-Powell, 2015). An example of this kind of adaptive or social challenge might be the teacher who is being asked to use new instructional techniques but feels that if he implemented the new techniques, he might now find himself unsettled by the idea that the previous techniques he used were not so effective (see Figure 5.1).

Figure 5.1   Two Frequently Occurring Resistance Catalysts

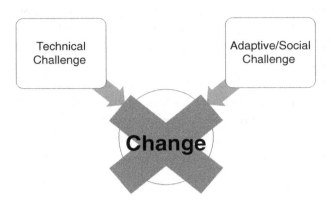

> The reason it is helpful for us to think about the kind of challenge that might be triggering the resistance is that the understanding of the challenge leads us to finding an appropriate response.

Either kind of challenge can push back against the change, as shown in Figure 5.1. Technical challenges and adaptive/social challenges are commonly found among people who are facing important changes in their work and schools. The reason it is helpful for us to think about the kind of challenge that might be triggering the resistance is that the understanding of the challenge leads us to finding an appropriate response. In other words, if people are met with responses that minimize their challenges, they might be willing to pursue the change with more dedication. The technical challenges and the resistance that results from them are more easily addressed by appropriate informational professional learning and time to practice the new procedures. Social/adaptive challenges are more complex. The error we often make is to assume that all upcoming change challenges, whether technical or social/adaptive, should be met by providing only information. Put another way, "One of the most common mistakes that schools or governments can make is trying to address an adaptive challenge with a technical solution" (Powell & Kusuma-Powell, 2015, p. 67).

Lawrence (1969) offers this perspective: "It may happen that there is some technical imperfection in the change that can readily be corrected. More than likely, it will turn out that the change is threatening and upsetting some of the established social arrangements for doing work" (p. 8). As he points out, whether or not the issue contributing to resistance is easy or difficult, leaders should know the kind of challenge that they are dealing with. To put it simply, if it is essentially a technical challenge and people are resistant to it because of a lack of information, it is simply logical to provide that information. As our experts have pointed out, however, it is not usually so simple. Often the technical challenges for the resistance may appear to be primary, but there might be a social challenge that is making the resistance more complicated. Let me give you an example.

> Again, years ago, I worked to supervise high schools in a very affluent part of the Dallas/Ft. Worth area. One of the high schools had a history of great academic and athletic success, and yet the math achievement scores of graduating high school students were not allowing them to achieve college course credit. To me, it seemed like a simple technical challenge—the high school math teachers might need to learn some newer instructional practices or dig deeper into their curriculum standards. I initiated conversations with the high school department chair, who seemed to understand the need for more professional learning with her teachers. Yet, when it was time for this professional learning to begin, she resisted all of my efforts to provide this.

In hindsight, I think the reason for her resistance was not simply that she and her teachers needed new information about teaching upper-level math (a technical challenge and solution). I believe that they resisted all of my efforts because I didn't recognize that my efforts were casting a light on their instructional practices and potentially either putting the spotlight on their deficiencies or causing them to lose credibility with their colleagues. The person most in danger of losing her credibility was the department chair, as she had been the chair for years and enjoyed quite a reputation and respect for her knowledge and authority, although her results were not that exceptional.

Jennifer Abrams (2009) gives us additional shades to the technical and adaptive challenges when she defines the reasons people may avoid the hard work and hard conversations. Her book *Having Hard Conversations* (2009) addresses those of us who have to regularly have those difficult conversations with others. For me, her work not only addresses the reasons we avoid those conversations but also why people avoid the hard work of change. A few of her reasons for this avoidance include the following:

Need for Personal Safety: Abrams (2009) reminds us that sometimes we are just anxious about the change or "we won't be able to hold ourselves steady" in the face of the hard work (p. 9). I believe her idea is directly related to the idea of a technical challenge. If taking on the change will submit a person to a threat of either emotional, social, or physical safety (Brown, 2017), it is entirely logical that he or she may avoid the change and resist implementing it altogether.

Need for Personal Comfort: I think of personal comfort to be similar to complacency. There are some cases where the need for personal comfort may be so strong that it just doesn't seem worth it to attempt the change (Abrams, 2009). A person who resists because of the need for personal comfort could be a professional just a few years from retirement, believing that he or she can "ride out" this change. I also think personal comfort may be related to the adaptive/social challenge for the person who resists the change because attempting the change would alter the social structure of the school and place the person in a new, less secure context.

Fear of the Unknown: Abrams (2009) suggests that this is the person who would "rather live with the status quo than take on the unknown" (p. 12). This fear could drive the person to be overt in his or her rejection of the change or simply try to fade into the background hoping not to be noticed. I believe the fear of the unknown may be directly related to the idea of a technical challenge. If the person fears that he or she doesn't have the skill or knowledge to attempt the change, it may seem better to simply avoid it because of the uncertainty of personal change accomplishment.

Conflict With Beliefs or Values: I remember that some of the Ashton Unified teachers implementing the reading program simply didn't think the new program was the right way to teach literacy to their students. This is an example of a conflict with beliefs or values, and an indication of a possible adaptive/ social challenge. Those same Ashton teachers went on to say (in the survey) that they just were not going to use it. Their rejection of the reading program shows how strong this conflict may be with professionals who view the forced change to a new program to be a "betrayal of the highest order" (Abrams, 2009, p. 22).

It is not earth-shattering to know that there is a myriad of reasons for the resistance of what seems to you to be an entirely logical change at your schools. For me, thinking about the technical and social/adaptive challenges sheds valuable light on the reason, which can trigger an appropriate response from me. Abrams (2009) lists many more reasons why we avoid hard and difficult conversations about changes than I highlighted here, and all are worthy to study. My thinking is that if we will not react to the resistance but rather respond to it when we have thought about the underlying reason for it, we might have more success in managing the resistance and even anticipating it. A handbook of strategies for addressing resistance follows in the next chapter.

Have Perspective on Why We Are Seeing So Much of It Now

As I have said before, the concept of dealing with resistance is probably the most frequent topic that I'm asked to address when I train current and future school leaders. I believe the reason we are seeing so many pockets of resistance is that we have actually led school change in a way that abolishes autonomy and diminishes professional voice, leaving people with fewer ways to vocalize their beliefs, preferred behaviors, and concerns. For years, we have reduced teacher autonomy and tried to "inspect quality" into our changes, carefully structuring it, prescribing curriculum, and assessing the quality of implementation with one measure: student achievement.

Teachers in classrooms know that significant change happens over time and is supported in buildings by effective principals who understand the change. Yet, change may have been mandated by leaders who apparently believe that it can be effectively implemented in a year or less. When the results are not great and there is pushback, those same leaders get nervous and search for the next new solution to their problems. Bechtle (2012) explains it this way: "When we're immersed in a culture of instant gratification, patience isn't our default setting. We've trained it right out of our lives. As a result, we're more easily irritated when people don't change. Often, people do change, but it doesn't happen overnight" (p. 123). So, really, we may notice so much resistance now because of us—we have been the problems, trying to implement change in ways that simply don't work. Teachers are smart and have become suspicious of "the next new thing."

There is another reason, I think, for so much resistance nowadays. The sense of autonomy is an important motivator for people, propelling them into the change and sustaining their motivating through the change (Pink, 2009). During change, people want a sense of acting with choice and they desire to live in a school context that represents a creative tension between the need to have structure and the ability to exercise personal freedom (Tschannen-Moran & Tschannen-Moran, 2010). Our ways of orchestrating change haven't allowed that balance between freedom and structure/control. We generally handle change by tipping the scale to the control side, attempting to drive the quality from our point of view and not inviting teachers to belong to a mutual community of appreciation, learning, support, and risk taking.

This lack of patience, ignorance of the need for a balance between freedom and structure, and our ill-conceived strategies of driving change, then, distort our view of what is happening in front of us. People may be voicing genuine concerns, but the pressure we are under prevents us from wanting to hear them. Instead, we "use every tactic you can think of—including distorting what your opponent the (resister) has said—in order to win the argument" (Tannen, 1998, p. 5). The idea of the change as having two sides—one is for the change, and the other is against—is problematic in itself. Tannen (1998) reminds us that the issue of change is not often composed of two opposing sides but a "crystal of many sides" (p. 10). She reminds us that often the truth and the pathway to change is in what she called a "complex middle," not a set of oversimplified opposing extremes. An outgrowth of this attitude may be that the people who are being asked to implement the change may feel more and more unheard and cut off than ever (Tannen, 1998).

Legitimize the Concerns They Are Sharing With You

The very people we may be irritated with because of their lack of progress or their refusal to embrace change are the ones most critical to the change's success.

One step toward organizational health is to want to hear and understand what people are saying about the change. The fact of the matter is that the very people we may be irritated with because of their lack of progress or their refusal to embrace the change are the ones most critical to the change's success. They are likely to have worries or concerns about the change, whether technical ("I can't do it") or adaptive/social ("How will this affect me here?"). They may be encountering legitimate hurdles or issues as they move from learning about it, to planning for it, to implementing the change. If these hurdles are not addressed, they may have a debilitating effect and derail the most carefully planned initiatives.

Hall and Hord (2001) call these concerns "Stages," which "give us a way of thinking about people's feelings and perceptions about change" (p. 57). These concerns may range from wanting more information about the change, to wondering how the change will personally affect them, to wanting to enact the change efficiently, to wanting the change to have more of an impact on their students.

Assessing these concerns about the change is vital to the planning and management of the change. The most practical way to assess individual concerns is through the "one-legged conversation" mentioned several times here and detailed in chapter 2, on initiation. Essentially, these conversations are deceptively simple—to find out what a teacher concern about the change might be, we just ask one question, which sounds like this when I use this technique:

> *"Think about our work to implement (name the change). When you think about it, what are your concerns? What are you worried about?"*

This question is asked in an informal setting, one-on-one with the teacher. When I'm using this strategy, I do not write down her comments while the teacher is telling me what she is concerned about. Instead, I just listen, probe, and paraphrase (writing down her concerns may cause the teacher to think that I will use her comments in her evaluation). When the teacher seems to be finished, I continue to ask her for more information, until she appears to have completely explained her concern to me. I conclude the conversation by thanking the teacher for her candor and assuring her that I will use what she told me to better support the implementation of the change.

Asking the question is the easy part—and it will build trust with the teacher if you are quiet and probe for your understanding. The hard part may be to refrain from quickly solving issues so the changes can move on. If we believe that real change is people change, then honoring people and their concerns is paramount. Therefore, I try not to solve the teacher's issues too quickly; that may give her the feeling that the problem she was encountering was not that significant and could be easily solved. Instead, I want to reflect on her comments and tell her that—and will use my understanding and the conversations with other people to help me really frame my responses to their issues.

This informal interview strategy will work if you and the teacher have a pretty solid and trusting relationship. Let's suppose that you ask several teachers on one day how they are feeling about the change and what their concerns are. After soliciting concerns from teachers, it will be time for a response to support the implementation and to prevent the stalling of effort. The chart in Figure 5.2 shows some of the possible concerns from Hall and Hord's research (2001) and some general ideas of how to respond to the concern.

Figure 5.2   Resolving Concerns

Four Types of Concerns Implementers May Have	What Might Be Done to Address the Concern
Information Concerns	Provide clear, consistent, and accurate information about the innovation.
Sounds like: "I'm not sure I understand this. I'd like to learn more before I can really commit to doing it well."	Use a variety of ways to share information—verbally, in writing, and through any available media. Communicate with individuals and with small and large groups.

Have people who have used the innovation successfully visit with your teachers. Schedule visits to other schools using the innovation.

Help teachers see how the innovation relates to their current practices, how it fits in nicely with what they already know.

Be enthusiastic and enhance the visibility of others who are using the innovation and are excited about it. |
| **Personal Concerns** | Legitimize the existence and expression of personal concerns. Express your own personal knowledge that these concerns are common. |
| *Sounds like:* "I look at all that will be required of me and I have to wonder, where will I start? This change seems so complicated and there are so many pieces to it. Can I do it?" | Use notes and personal comments to reinforce the person's personal adequacy to handle the change.

Emphasize and highlight short-term successes with the innovation.

Connect concerned teachers with others whose personal concerns have diminished and who will be supportive.

Show how the innovation can be achieved by taking it in short segments.

Do not push the innovation use, but encourage and support it while maintaining the vision and expectations for gradual implementation. |
| **Management Concerns** | Clarify the steps and components of the innovation. |
| *Sounds like:* "I can't seem to get all of it done in the time I have. It's taking so long for me to write the lesson plans!" | Provide answers that address the small specific "how to" issues that are so often the cause of management concerns.

Demonstrate exact and practical solutions to the logistical problems that are hindering the innovation. |

	Pair teachers with others who have dealt with the management concerns.
	Use faculty gatherings to brainstorm common management dilemma solutions.
	Attend to the immediate demands perceived by teachers, not the ultimate future vision.
Consequence Concerns	Provide these individuals with opportunities to visit other settings where the innovation is in use or to attend conferences on the topic.
Sounds like:	Give these individuals positive support and feedback and point out how the innovation is affecting students (when in classrooms).
"I can see the results with my students now. I'm looking to see how it might even support them better. Some of my students still need some content that the program doesn't provide."	Use walkthroughs and learning walks to look for enhanced engagement of students and point out to these teachers.
	Find opportunities for these people to share their skills with others.

Examples of appropriate responses may help. For instance, a teacher may be trying to implement a new reading program (like Ashton Unified School District schools) and says,

> *"I'm really trying, Mike. I have all of the materials but I'm so frustrated that I now have so many materials to use that I can't get it all in during my scheduled time. I can't quite seem to get them all planned out so the kids are successful. It's crazy, but on some days I just omit parts of the program because I can't figure out how to use it."*

This teacher is not, at the present time, resisting the change—on the contrary, she is trying to do it and do it well. In her mind, "doing it well" means getting all of the components taught efficiently during her allotted time each day. Her concerns at this moment are not on her students and their learning; instead, they are focused on her own management of the change and the program materials. If her concern is mainly and most significantly on management of the change, then if the management concerns are not helped, she might eventually abandon the change and becoming a resister because "it's too hard to implement." She needs to be supported in figuring out how to combine all of her materials into a coherent sequence of instruction. As a school leader, I'm thrilled that she has shared this information with me; and because I now have clarity on the issues, I do not have to spend time trying to read her mind to see the problem. The specific understanding can lead me to do something about the issue, and my action may preemptively decrease the possibility of her resistance, addressing the issues before they become too overwhelming for her.

Know That Words and Actions Matter When Addressing Resistance

Asking people for their concerns is relatively easy, but it is relatively hard to avoid some of the common reactions we may have to their concerns. First, it may be really hard for you not to fix the problem or issues on the spot. I have found that being thoughtful, asking questions, and requesting some time to think about the concern he or she has goes a long way in building trust with that person. I'm not saying that you wouldn't ever address the concern; on the contrary, you *must* address the issue that becomes evident as a result of these informal conversations. And yet, you want people to know that you have really thought about an appropriate response before you jump to a knee-jerk reaction. Second, the language that is used when asking the question is so important. You want to be as open-ended as possible, not offering your opinion but seeking an understanding of the person. Your purpose in having these frequent conversations is to learn their perspectives, not use the time as a chance to "sell" your change to them. It may seem counterintuitive, but you will gain a lot more in leading the change by listening to the people who are attempting it.

As Tannen (1998) reminds us, the words you use and the manner in which you say them really do matter. She says that "when we think we are using language, language is using us" (p. 14). The words "invisibly mold our way of thinking about people, actions, and the world around us" (p. 14). That is why the savvy leader carefully asks questions and then intuitively steps back and uses words to learn more so he or she is not operating from assumptions. "If I can know the truth, I could have made better assumptions and experienced different emotions. In fact, that's exactly what happens when I finally discover the truth" (Bechtle, 2012, p. 27).

So, words and the approach can either help dispel false assumptions about the resistance or reinforce accusatory, false assumptions we ignorantly hold. As we have said before, one of the most effective conversations will be built on the foundation of the teacher's level of trust with you, the vision of what we want to achieve, the intent of the conversation, and the teacher's degree of expertise with the change that we are talking about (Tomlinson & Murphy, 2015).

> Your purpose in having these frequent conversations is to learn their perspectives, not use the time as a chance to "sell" your change to them.

There is also the fact that we all tend to lead these conversations from the viewpoint of our personal, most comfortable style. This style of leading and conversing is influenced by our own comfort level—for instance, how comfortable are you asking questions and supporting the thinking of others? Or are you more comfortable soliciting information and then making a well-informed decision yourself? You and I have taken our fair share of leadership "style" inventories, and yet in practice, when supporting change, the most effective leader seems to be one who is fluid, moving along a continuum of words and behaviors. These leaders, I believe, reduce resistance because they are matching their style of leading with what is needed at that moment. Consider Figure 5.3, a very simple continuum of leadership style preferences, adapted from the Learning Forward Texas Leadership Development Process training (Texas Leadership Center, 1999).

What seems to matter is "the leader's knowledge of his or her own preferred style and the willingness to be fluid along the continuum, based on the contextual factors and knowledge about the individual he or she wishes to engage" (Tomlinson & Murphy, 2015, p. 101). For instance, a teacher may need some direction and, based on what she is saying, may need to learn more about the change before she starts using it. In that case, a "command" style is probably what that person needs—some direction from you in order to strengthen her skill set. At another time, your most effective style may be to coach a teacher who is struggling with the implementation but appears to have a full grasp of the innovation, and your intuition tells you she already knows what action she should take.

Figure 5.3   Leadership Preference Continuum

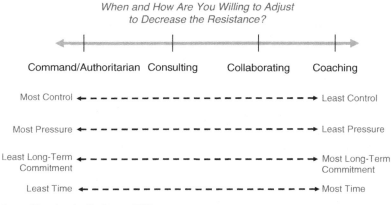

Source: Texas Leadership Center, 1999.

You sense, in that latter example, that it would be most useful for you to ensure that she can spend a few minutes being reflective on her skills.

I would say that one of the most valuable leadership skills, then, is for you to be fully aware—aware of the way you go about your business, the way you conduct conversations, and your patience with the change—and then, acting on this knowledge. Often, the issues or concerns hindering implementation may seem completely unfounded to you. While they may appear irrational from your perspective, believe it—they are real for the people feeling them. It's probably wise to always remember Ariely's reminder that "understanding irrationality is important for our everyday actions and decisions, and for understanding how we design our environment" (Ariely, 2008, p. xix). Hargreaves and Fullan (2012) would add, "Know your people and understand their culture" (p. 164). Fluidity in leading can lead to the anticipation and reduction of the issues that might spark some formidable resistance later if not addressed.

Consider Carefully the Consequences Before Acting

In order to cultivate the kinds of deep changes that we seek, we must orchestrate a set of actions and supports that both expect teachers to grow and support their growth by addressing concerns and meeting needs. It is seductive to begin looking at school improvement as a complex set of action plans. While action plans may map out the changes, the real change will occur when the focus is on the people who work in the school—this focus on both results and relationships becomes the effective leader's mantra and guidance for everyday actions.

Every school leader feels an urgency for deep, lasting change. Along the journey from initiation to institutionalization of a productive change, the leader will see the pockets of resistance—usually triggered by one if not several of the reasons we have detailed in this chapter. It's really useful to remember that resistance often happens for a reason; our job is not to stop it, but rather, to learn from it and address it. Dealing with resistance mirrors the characteristics of the empathetic leader. The goal—understanding and demonstrating empathy—is distinctly different from demonstrating sympathy. As leaders, we need to be empathetic to the issues of resistance but at the same time be determined to achieve our results. I believe that this definition of empathy serves us well as we think about when or if to respond to the issues that may be driving us crazy. That definition is "seeking to both understand a person's condition from their perspective and understand the needs of others, with the aim of acting to make a difference in responding to those needs or building on the positives" (Tomlinson & Murphy, 2018).

> As leaders, we need to be empathetic to the issues of resistance but at the same time be determined to achieve our results.

There is a warning about acting on the resistance. Jennifer Abrams (2009) reminds us that "it isn't a good idea to speak up every time or in every situation that you see something you feel is wrong" (p. 27). Sometimes, the resistance is actually part of the teacher's growth, development, and struggle as he is incorporating the change into his repertoire. By supporting him and leaning into his concerns, implementation issues often resolve themselves with steady leadership, a listening ear, and motivation. Occasionally, however, the leader must speak up and address resistance that she feels is in direct opposition to the vision of the school and its undergirding beliefs. Abrams identifies "categories of questions to ask yourself" (2009) that she has gleaned from Debra Meyerson (2001). These categories of reflective questions have been influential to me and incredibly useful to consider before you act. It makes sense to share three of them with you as we think about our own timing of resistance intervention. After each category, note my personal comments.

Timing

- Is it the right time to rely on the relationship you have (hopefully) built and speak your mind?

- Will the problem fix its own if I support it by addressing the person's concerns?

- How intense is the issue?

- How am I feeling about this issue? How emotional am I?

- Do I have all of the information I need in order to respond effectively?

My personal thoughts: I often found that my own emotions often were my worst enemy when I was formulating a response. When I was leading schools, I often thought that every time was the right time for me to speak up and address the issue. This was not the case. Sometimes, the person was just voicing concerns and I misunderstood them for downright resistance. If I had addressed the concerns and supported the person while maintaining our vision, I believe the resistance would have naturally gone away. Instead, when I chose to respond and was emotional about it, I found that I made the situation worse.

Stakes

- What is the worst thing and the best thing that can happen as a result of my response?

- Is this a discussion worth having right now?

- Who else might this conversation I'm about to have be affected by it? What will be the ripple effect?

- Is there something dangerous about the behavior that forces me to respond?

My personal thoughts: It's imperative to consider how important the issue is or whether or not the issue might cause damage to others or students. I often found that it helped me to actually put the issue on a scale from "minimally important" to "incredibly important" and reflect on that before I responded. In addition, we often think that the issue of resistance belongs to the individual person; it often does, but frequently your response may have an impact on either the culture of the school or others whose relationships are vital to you and your initiatives.

Options

- Who should initiate the conversation?

- Should I bring the information to someone else more appropriate to handle it?

- Will my response somehow jeopardize my credibility and trust with this person?

- Have I tried to bring this issue up before and my approach didn't work?

- Should the issue be discussed using another medium besides face-to-face?

My personal thoughts: I'm a fan of face-to-face conversations, because I learn from the body language the person is using as well as the actual words. If my preferred way of communicating isn't possible, then the question becomes "How can I have the conversation in a way that builds trust and the relationship while squarely focusing on the issue at hand?" In addition, sometimes, the issue is affecting other people, members of the person's team, or trusted colleagues. They may be the people more effective in addressing the issue, or perhaps the issue is one that is held by the part of the team. I always had to pay attention to the words I was going to use when addressing the issue, because I found that my words, although unintentional, sometimes betrayed my purpose or objective and diminished the trust that person and I felt with each other.

Deciding to act on the resistance is a bit more complicated than we think. There are repercussions to our actions, as we often find out after it's too late. Time can be our friend, as we are considering whether or not to act on an issue that we worry may derail our progress. I often found that when I was really feeling the urge to react to the resistance, I needed to wait—and take some time to understand it so I could *respond* to it rather than react. Patterson, Grenny, Maxfield, McMillan, and Switzler (2013) summarize the leader's considerations before acting on resistance: "First, you have to take the time to unbundle the problem. People are often in too much of a hurry to do this. Their emotions propel them to move quickly, and speed rarely leads to careful thought. Second, while sorting through the issues, you have to decide what is bothering you the most. If you don't, you will end up going after either the wrong target or too many targets. Third, you have to be concise. You have to distill the issue to a single sentence. If you can't reduce a violation [the resistance issue] to a clear sentence before you talk, the issue almost never becomes more understandable and focused as a conversation unfolds" (pp. 24–25).

Don't Make the Issue Worse

In this chapter, we have seen that our leadership "style" is important as we lead change from initiation to deep institutionalization, or permanence. The key in understanding our natural leadership style preferences is to also recognize that in different contexts and with different people, we have to adjust our style of leading in order to support individuals more fully. To put it another way, being fixed in our styles may actually make the resistance worse. Take an example: If our natural style is more command than anything else, we really value the idea of speaking to the change and attempting to either convince people of the better idea or demand compliance. If not kept checked, this fixed style may actually deepen and perpetuate resistance. Kerry Patterson and his coauthors remind us that "raw power, painfully applied, may move bodies, it may even get people to act in new ways, but it rarely moves hearts and minds" (Patterson et al., 2013, p. 110). As we have learned, for something to be institutionalized into the school's fabric, it has to appeal to the purpose of the school and give people a sense of deep satisfaction that this is the right thing to do. Institutionalization banks on "moving hearts and minds." So, while a fixed command style may lead to temporary changes, it will rarely lead to changes that are internalized.

Really, a "fixed" way of leading is akin to the "fixed" mindset (Dweck, 2006), which contributes to a faulty thinking about growth and progress. When a leader holds a fixed mindset about the resistance he is seeing, it removes him from the possibility of learning from it—instead, he just wants it to go away and attributes the resistance to some kind of inadequacy in the other individual. This may lead him to a refusal to examine the resistance and simply exert more positional power to make the resistance go away. Again, there are repercussions to this attitude. "Every time we decide to use our power to influence others, particularly if we're gleeful or hasty, we damage the relationship" (Patterson et al., 2013, p. 114). As we have seen, our focus has to be bifocal—resting on both a focus on the results we must have *and* the relationships with people as our agents of that change. The use of our position to force the change and the failure that will inevitably result in that command approach will just make our bewilderment even worse as we blame the lack of change on others and refuse to reflect on our own actions.

Strategize and Implement a Productive Conversation With the Resister

Let's say that you see pockets of resistance and you have taken the time to carefully consider any response on your part. Upon reflection, you have decided to have that tough conversation and try to (a) address the resistance, (b) understand it more fully, and (c) reinforce a commitment to the purpose of the change while helping the individual see the path ahead. While there are no absolute right ways and wrong ways to have that conversation, there are, again, some important considerations:

Think about the logistics. Harley (2013) reminds us that the conversation should almost always be in private. "If you want to guarantee that someone will get defensive, give her feedback in front of other people or in a cubicle where it's almost certain others can hear the conversation. The recipient will be so embarrassed or worried that others are listening that she won't hear a thing you're saying and will immediately distrust you" (p. 135). Therefore, while considering the privacy of the feedback, also determine the location and the timing of the conversation.

Think about what you want to say. Remember Patterson and his coauthors' challenge to see if you can boil the issue down into one sentence. This will force you to be succinct and clarify what the issue really is. Narrowing the issue will also allow the person to focus on that area of improvement. Again, Harley reminds us that "people can't focus on ten things at a time" (Harley, 2013, p. 135). She instructs us to make the issue as small and focused as possible while still reinforcing the person's effort, acknowledging progress, and addressing those things that still must change (Harley, 2013).

Think about how you want the conversation to feel. After having so many of these conversations, I found that it was helpful to not only think of *what* I wanted to say but *how I wanted both of us to feel* during the conversation. I continue to believe that these tough conversations can both address the issues head on and maintain the trusting relationship I have worked so hard to facilitate. See Figure 5.4 for a representation of this kind of conversation strategy.

I need the conversation to be based on these three feelings:

- **Collaborative.** I want both of us to feel that there is real learning and an exchange of a point of view with each other.

- **Optimistic.** I need the conversation to feel positive and optimistic that a change can happen, and that change will be within the person's grasp if I work to provide the right support.

- **Experimental.** I must convey a sense of experimentation, and want both of us to feel that we can consider new ideas and commit to trying them out without negative, personal impact.

When we reviewed the three phases of change from initiation to institutionalization, we focused, in part, on what people need during that phase. Addressing the needs and soliciting concerns was a part of the effective leader's repertoire as we simultaneously work to sustain the change and address any challenges along the way. As a school principal

Figure 5.4   A Productive Conversation

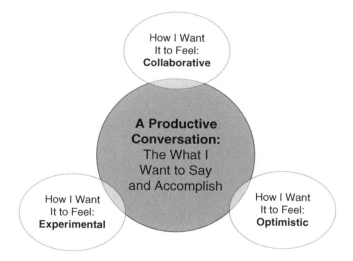

and district leader, I found that being proactive and anticipating the issues and concerns *before* they popped up needed to be one of my key habits as I worked every day. There are some predictable triggers of resistance; while there are no right ways and wrong ways to address resistance, there are some vital considerations for us. Before acting on the resistance, these actions must be carefully considered as we respond to the issue. In the next chapter, we will look at specific strategies that you may want to employ, matched to both the issue and pertinent considerations. While these strategies will not form a recipe book for each of us, they may give you some ideas you had not thought about. We will also look more deeply into how both the Kingsport City Schools leaders and the Ashton Unified School District leaders both anticipated resistance and dealt with it.

But for now, let's again pause and analyze our responses to these questions that seem to describe the complexities of resistance and how we handle it.

Take a Moment

In thinking about the way I handle resistance, to what extent do I

- understand my own emotions that I often feel when I see resistance;

- know my own comfort level with resistance;

- see examples of both the technical challenges and the adaptive/social challenges that often trigger resistance;

- identify issues of safety in my school culture and work to decrease those issues;

- believe that some resistance is actually legitimate;

- show my confidence in asking people what their concerns or issues might be;

- adjust my preferred leadership style to better match my approach to what people are needing;

- consider timing, the stakes, and options before acting on resistance;

- think about not only what I want to say to the resister but also how I want both of us to feel during the conversation; and

- make sure that all of my tough conversations reinforce the results that we are trying to achieve and the relationships that we are building?

OUR TWO SCHOOL DISTRICTS AND THE ATTEMPTS TO MANAGE THE RESISTANCE

We have been reminded that most of us will experience pockets of resistance while we are leading necessary changes. Leaders in Kingsport City Schools and the Ashton Unified School District certainly did. Yet, those leaders in our two districts reacted and responded to the forms of resistance in differing ways. Their responses achieved some success. As you might suspect, Kingsport City Schools experienced less overt resistance, and the resistance they did address seemed much more manageable. They also seemed to be "out front" of the resistance. Because of their decisive actions, those Kingsport leaders seemed to handle the resistance in a way that honored the resisters while simultaneously pushing for compliance. The Ashton Unified School District leaders, in contrast, seemed regularly surprised by the resistance that occurred. Their responses tended to feel more like quick reactions or well-intentioned efforts that fell short because of the trust issues that prevailed.

Kingsport City Schools

The Kingsport City Schools leaders were methodical in their plans to implement a new kind of instructional coach in all of their schools. The name of the instructional coach was changed, a large amount of time was spent on professional learning for the coaches, and principals were brought in early to form a partnership of school leader and instructional coach.

Even though the change was methodically planned, there was some resistance to the transition. The first signs of any resistance appeared when the InDeS were on site at the first part of the school year. The resistance came, actually, from the InDeS themselves! These coaches had been trained in the purest form of instructional coaching and were ready to change the world. When they began that first year in their schools, they found that teachers were asking them to provide resources and accomplish tasks that were not particularly impactful. The InDeS voiced open intolerance toward these kinds of menial tasks at their monthly coaching meetings. In addition, remember that the InDeS were asked to log their time at first and specify what kind of support they were giving the teachers (as a part of the first-year assessment of effectiveness). InDeS were not particularly excited about doing this as well. They saw the act as pulling them away from more important kinds of

(Continued)

(Continued)

support with their teachers. Again, they were quite comfortable voicing their feelings about this requirement (which I thought was a good thing). It was important that Kingsport City Schools district officials were in close contact with the InDeS during initiation and the early part of implementation. These district leaders chose an interactive style with the InDeS that was more collaborative and did not force compliance; rather, they listened to concerns and sought to explain the larger purpose for their on-site requests. This strategy seemed to work. When InDeS understood the larger rationale, they were generally accepting of the requests as short-term inconveniences. I still admire the district leaders for taking this approach. It demonstrated to the InDeS that they were equal partners in this venture and forged a level of trust in the process.

During initiation, or the start of any change, people are hungry for the purpose, want to know how the change will personally affect them, and need to have as much information as they can to build their understanding of the change. Even though Kingsport leaders were methodical in how they were approaching the new instructional coaching initiative, a lack of information and understanding dogged some of their efforts. Brian Cinnamon explains: "Principals didn't fully understand the roles of InDeS as they were working in the schools. We decided we needed to stay with our design and create the capacity of individuals to do key work—stick to what we felt was the role of the InDeS. Where there was less school-based leadership, InDeS were not necessarily being used in the desired way." Ashley Carter, one of the original InDeS, agrees with Cinnamon's assessment: "I think [the district leaders] gave principals the knowledge about the new form of coaching, but I don't know if much time was spent on what the role is as much as they did with this is what the role is not."

That predominant feeling among Kingsport school principals was that they needed some instructional help at their schools, and yet when asked to create working "contracts" with their InDeS, which described this kind of instructional help, some of them balked. They did not voice open hostility to the idea; instead, several of them simply looked at the contract as a "task they had to complete" and didn't put much effort into it, frustrating those InDeS. This was a case of *reluctance*—which I think of as a first cousin of resistance—because both reluctance and resistance have virtually the same effect. This reluctance to complete the contract and describe the kind of specific instructional help that would elevate their schools might have been intensified by the principals' need for more guidance and information about the vision for the role of the InDeS.

District leaders supported their principals through this requirement in differentiated ways. Again, it may have been for some leaders a daunting task because they were not confident about their own instructional knowledge or how to use the InDeS effectively. It could have been that it was also seen as a useless task, consuming way more time than desired. For whatever reason, district leaders decided that each principal's needs must be taken into account, and they acted accordingly with appropriate "heat" and "light" to get the job done effectively.

The majority of the time in implementation was without major, organized resistance. Because InDeS were asked to provide a variety of supports at the beginning of implementation, teachers were able to use them in a wide variety of ways. While some of these ways may not have exactly pleased the InDeS, they tolerated the wide range of effective requests. During the second and third years, they found that they had built enough trust in teachers to gently move them toward more impactful partnerships.

You may be surmising that this implementation went without a hitch for the most part, and you are correct. It did take some hard work and specific anticipatory actions, however. Even though at the time of this publication, the district is completing its fourth year of the InDeS transition, there are still nagging concerns that the use of InDeS could get derailed by other initiatives. For instance, there are other planning initiatives in place now in Kingsport that, if not carefully integrated into their planning "whole," might either drown or alter the InDeS role. Also, all three of my interviewees voiced a need to deepen the work—diving into more impactful work with teachers and continuing to deepen the knowledge and the skills of the InDeS themselves.

To summarize, the implementation and institutionalization of the InDeS had little drama because district officials had their ears to the ground, listening for sounds of dissatisfaction. In addition, having regular monthly meetings with the InDeS kept the communication at a maximum and the size of the problems at a minimum. Principals waxed and waned in their use of the InDeS and some continued to be unconvinced as to the best use of their coach; however, the entire implementation moved along, and by the third and fourth years, principals voiced more confidence that the InDeS were critical to the success of their schools. The savvy Kingsport leaders didn't rest on what seemed to be an overall smooth implementation, however. They are still searching for ways to make the work of the InDeS more impactful and are mindful of possible competing and conflicting initiatives.

(Continued)

(Continued)

Key illustrations of how the Kingsport City Schools sustained their change to instructional coaching while managing resistance include the following:

- They realized that the InDeS themselves were critical partners and encouraged free, open communication with them when issues of InDeS dissatisfaction appeared.

- They acknowledged that some of the early InDeS tasks did not match with the InDeS vision of instructional coaching (see Abrams, 2009, in the previous chapter discussing a "conflict in beliefs") but reminded the coaches of the purpose and the short-term aspects of the tasks.

- Concerns were legitimized, not suppressed.

- They brought principals into the conversation early in implementation, and while they required some tasks and products that produced some resistance, they handled the resistance in differentiated ways.

- They maintained a balance of "heat and light," requiring some products and behaviors while delivering effective support for the initiative. This gave some comfort to both the InDeS and the principals during the years of implementation.

- They anticipated ways to deepen the InDeS work and are working to align all new initiatives with the work of the InDeS.

The Ashton Unified School District

Leaders in the Ashton Unified School District were convinced that the current K–5 reading program in their district wasn't working. Students were not performing as expected on state examinations, and teachers were routinely communicating the inadequacy of the existing curriculum to their school principals, local union representatives, and district leaders. Members of the school board were also displeased with student reading performance and were urging the new superintendent and her staff to make a change. After some research, a new reading program was selected and the initiation and implementation of that program was launched.

In Ashton, there was certainly a need for new reading materials and a fairly unified mindset that a change would bring relief to both teachers and students. Yet, almost from the very start of initiation, there were problems. My feeling is that it stemmed from two things: a lack of time with and understanding of the new reading program before implementation and an unclear system of supporting the implementation of the materials at the classroom level.

Teacher training on the new materials was spotty and rather unfocused, and yet the first group of those K–2 teachers was expected to use the new materials after very little experience with the materials before the start of that school year. I believe that those inadequately prepared teachers, in a good-faith effort to comply, essentially "made up" how the materials were to be used. The materials were then not uniformly used and, in some cases, teachers were picking and choosing which activities and materials they liked, leading to a fragmentation of the components of balanced literacy. As the saying goes, it was like teachers were building their planes (their understanding of the reading curriculum) while trying to fly them (teach the reading curriculum on a daily basis).

This lack of information and experiences with the new reading materials led to the overt resistance district officials heard early in the initiation year. As teachers were attempting to sort the issues out, district leaders began a general piling on of "help." Diane Connelly, Ashton union representative, describes the "help" in this way: "Instructional coaches were brought into place during that same year (the K–2 teachers), and the teachers didn't know the coaches' role in anything; the preassessment of the students that was required during the first two months of that first year wasn't appropriate; people told me that the training had been inadequate; the program seemed rigid and prescriptive; there was concern about how much time all of the planning was going to take; grade-level planning was now being prescribed for a specific time in the day and the coach would be involved in those meetings. There was a lot of content and there was uncertainty about how much teachers had to cover and what they had to cover."

The district leaders had decided that the instructional coaches could help in the implementation; and yet, the coaches were also new to their roles and were trying to figure that out while being told that they were critical to the reading implementation. Debra Olson, a district leader directly working with the change, described how she felt that she was playing "catch-up" with the coaches and continues to do so even now. Many of the coaches did not have expertise in reading, which made the catch-up even more challenging. As coaches wrestled with their roles and this new curriculum, many were influenced by their school leaders to assume roles with teachers that were not trust building. Several of my interviewees talked about coaches becoming "implementation police," which altered their role of collaborator and supporter of teachers.

(Continued)

(Continued)

The straw that may have broken the implementation's back might have been the development of Priority Plans, curriculum maps of sorts that were designed to drive daily instruction and give specific guidance to teachers as to the pacing of the content. Teachers had actually asked for some kind of planning guidance, and the plans were a response to that request. However, it may have been the *how* of the plans that got in the way, not the plans themselves. In other words, the plans themselves appeared to be thorough and well-developed. It was the *delivery* of the plans that seemed to cause such great dissatisfaction with teachers. It appeared that all of a sudden, the plans removed any teacher autonomy from instructional delivery. While teachers had asked for guidance, they had *not* asked for strict adherence to a recipe that didn't allow for any variation in content, process, or product.

All of these issues contributed to widespread dissatisfaction and resistance by large numbers of teachers who were supposed to be implementing and appreciating the new reading curriculum. While at the time of this publication, the district is fully into implementation of the K–5 program, it is still experiencing resistance from teachers and principals, who may not know how to lead reading instruction at their schools. There had been general agreement that new reading approaches were needed. What seemed to get leaders into trouble was a series of unorganized measures to "launch" the program. In short, district leaders underestimated the importance of proper initiation. For this reason, they continue to try to quiet disruptive resistance while moving forward, and the numbers and severity of the issues continued to pile on, hampering the change. It seemed to me that district leaders were operating with a general lack of understanding about the *how* of change leadership. Those same district leaders, however, were eager to solve the issues and attempted to level out the resistance. Yet, their actions were often made in silos without regard to others affected by the outcomes of their decisions. For instance, district leaders often made decisions that they thought would help implementation without realizing the impact their decisions would have on principals and/or instructional coaches.

Ashton district leaders, however, have continued to work at it. They continue to put into place some measures to manage the resistance and reset their reading initiative. Key illustrations of how the Ashton Unified School District leaders have adjusted in their change to a new reading program while managing resistance include the following:

- They are now working more closely with building principals to not only build their understanding of quality reading but also support their skills in leading the change at their buildings.

- The Priority Plans are being adjusted in terms of format. In addition, each Priority Plan identifies the "non-negotiables" and "negotiables" for teachers to follow.

- Training for instructional coaches continues to build their understanding of reading.

- The district leadership and union leadership are now publishing a joint communique on a regular basis that details the progress the district is making in its implementation.

- The district has now adopted a rigorous program assessment scheme, requiring the district to regularly collect varieties of formative data to use for overall reading implementation discussion, analysis, interpretation, and adjustments.

The Ashton Unified School District leaders knew that they needed a more powerful reading curriculum as well as instructional strategies that aligned with that curriculum. The lack of a patient and strategic initiation plan led to the development of issues early on. Fragmented reactions to resolve those issues led to even more deeply held dissatisfaction among teachers. District leaders were seen as unresponsive or responsive in ways that were not beneficial. Problems were not a result of a lack of leadership caring or effort. Ashton leaders worked hard at getting out in front of the implementation, and yet they were confronted by problems around every corner. It could be that their impatience for change was their worst enemy. Efforts to coordinate "help" at the school level, because they were not aligned among instructional coaches and principals, led to more confusion and a lack of widespread support of the change.

Persistence may be Ashton's best friend in this implementation—if that persistence is coupled with (a) listening to concerns, (b) coordinating efforts among key implementation supporters (coaches and principals), and (c) regular assessment, interpretation, and resolution of issues. District leaders cannot be criticized for their intent. Again, the *what* of the change in Ashton has not been as troublesome as the *how* the change has been orchestrated.

CHAPTER 6

STRATEGIES FOR UNDERSTANDING AND MANAGING THE PUSHBACK

Learn from the resistance and use a strategy that maintains focus and honors a different point of view.

KEY PRACTICE

Embrace the Unpleasantness, but Embrace It Calmly and Strategically

My natural tendency is to approach my work in schools in almost a clinical way—examining the issues, understanding the conditions, working for solutions, and assessing progress. The danger in this approach is that it may be too unbalanced for what people need where I'm working. I can get so caught up in the work that I might unconsciously ignore the issues that people might be having with the change. I have spent a lot of years in school leadership, and this realization has been both powerful, unsettling, and useful to me. The recognition that I do this is powerful—my own reflection of my approach and my mindset is useful as I balance my natural desire for results with my understanding of the richness and complexity of the people who are doing the work with me. It is unsettling because it reminds me of how I approached some issues in previous schools with such tenacity that I didn't see how my leadership was actually eroding the relationships that were so vital in actualizing the changes we needed.

I have to also admit that resistance to the change can be rather irritating to me, and I often find it hard to take the time to conceptualize *why* the resistance is happening. Once again, being aware of this tendency is valuable as it helps me consciously guard against my biased approach. When leading our endeavors, it's wise not to make the common mistake of expecting resistance to happen, as it may not. But more often than not, the implementation of the change will encounter some unexpected challenges that might contribute to a dissatisfaction of the work in others. When this happens, it is our job to seek information and understanding about the resistance and act on behalf of the person and the situation, not ignore or suppress it. This effort may be hard for some of us; but as I have said before, folks a lot smarter than me have warned of the leadership pitfall of ignoring the problems or the people who seem to be causing them.

In her book *How to Hug a Porcupine*, Ellis (2009) refers to the "human porcupines" in our lives, prickly folks who seem to pop up in unexpected ways and circumstances and point out why things are not going as well as you wish. She describes it in this way: "No matter where you encounter a porcupine, whether you are meeting him for the first time or have known her for years, having some reliable strategies in your back pocket can make all the difference in the world. With knowledge and the right attitude on your side, you can not only make the best out of a bad situation, but, with practice, learn how to avoid painful spots altogether" (p. 11). As we have said throughout this book, resistance may happen in any phase of the change—the very beginning, during the rigors of implementation, or even years later when competing changes begin to erode the change you thought was well established. We have

seen how both of our school districts met resistance head on with varying levels of success. In large-scale change initiatives, leaders often must
focus on broad categories of timing, clarity, priority, communication,
professional learning, and support. For many of us, resistance appears
with individual people and demands a response from us. This chapter,
then, is an attempt to provide some reliable strategies that you can carry
in your back pocket. The strategies are grouped according to the type
of resistance you may be seeing. Study each of the strategies in the five
categories I have chosen and remember that each strategy has merit and
can be applied either in instances of individual resistance or broadened
to an overall approach to handle the anticipated pushback.

Resistance Issue: People Seem Interested and Capable, but Fail to Get Started

Strategy: Assess Whether It Is a Technical Issue or a Social/Adaptive Issue and Then Act on the Fear's Behalf.

In chapter 5, Lawrence (1969) pointed out two possible reasons or
contributing factors for the resistance. They include either (a) a technical fear or challenge and/or (b) a social/adaptive fear or challenge.
Again, consider Figure 6.1:

The *technical fear or challenge* results when there is vital information or skill that the person needs to move forward with the
change. His or her fear is that he will not acquire or be able to
use the required knowledge or skill in order to be successful. The
social/adaptive fear or challenge is the result of the worry that the
embracing of the new change will somehow alter the social relationships within the school.

Figure 6.1   Two Frequently Occurring Resistance Catalysts

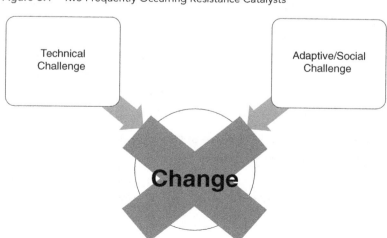

If we suspect that one or both of these fears are at play, then our work is to act on behalf of that fear. That means to understand the logic of the fear and then provide some kind of measure(s) that will diffuse the fear or build the person's confidence to take on the challenge of the change. For instance:

Example #1: If it is felt that the person might not believe he has the knowledge or skills to make the change (the technical fear or challenge), then two leadership actions are suggested. They are to (a) provide multiple opportunities and ways for the person to acquire that knowledge he needs—such as training, work with another individual or coach, or work with you to collaborate on plans; and (b) find ways for that person to begin the work in a small way to experience success. Our theory is that if the person feels more equipped with the knowledge or the skill required for the change and has a place to start (even if the start is rather small), then he will be more likely to stay with the change and try the next step.

Example #2: If it is felt that the person might be fearful that the new change will cause new relationships and a new social dynamic in the school or in her team (the social/adaptive fear), the needed leadership strategy is to understand the loss that the person might feel and reflect on the kinds of relationships that the person may be valuing, and then ensure that the push to embrace the change doesn't fragment what is valued by that individual. For instance, a department chair who has built a reputation for her leadership and teaching quality resists a new mathematics program, and it seems illogical to you. What may be at work is that the department chair has based her reputation on what has been happening and the success that the department has been feeling. The use of the new mathematics program, she fears, might be an admission that there has been a way to improve all along and she has not led her team to recognize it. In other words, she may fear that she will lose credibility and her reputation may suffer as a leader if the change is implemented. Again, our actions should support the kind of social relationships she wants to maintain. Our encouragement to use the new mathematics program might center on focusing on the purpose of the change but encourage her to lead her team to investigate innovative ways to implement it. The effect, then, is to retain leadership in her hands as much as possible because she values that and fears that the change may endanger what she values.

Strategy: Apply the Right Balance of "Heat" and "Light" to Support Positive Action of the Individual(s).

The right kind of pressure and support actually provides comfort for individuals attempting the change. For me, it is a balance

Figure 6.2   The Balance or Imbalance of Heat and Light

- Heat may provide guidance and direction for folks who are resisting the change.
- A partnership of heat and light is necessary to move the work forward.
- An imbalance of heat and light may contribute to resistance.

of the two. I also have found that an imbalance of the two may lead to "action paralysis"—the inability to get started (see Figure 6.2).

Heat is essentially pressure that we exert on people to use the change. There is nothing inherently wrong with pressure to use the change; in fact, a certain amount of pressure can be comforting to the individual as it provides clarity and direction—two concepts we all need to be successful in work. However, too much heat or pressure can also be debilitating to individuals—for it provides none of the support we also need. Support, then, is the feeling that people share that there are pathways for success and that the resources, schedules, professional learning, and conversations will build the kind of culture to value the change. Support, however, without a certain amount of heat, may be paralyzing. Too much support provides limited direction and not much clarity—under these conditions, people are also often "action paralyzed."

The strategy is simple, then. Our dialogue and actions must demonstrate a combination of both heat and light if people are to move forward with the change. Obviously, the combination of heat and light needed will vary according to the individual and the context. This combination of heat and light messages may be most often seen and heard through our conversations with the individual who is resisting. I can see myself saying something like this to the resister:

> *"Harold, the change to new math standards is important to us because it is part of our vision to support our students in better ways. So, the use of new standards is a non-negotiable for all of us. I want to know how you will get started using these standards. But I also want to know how you want to do that and what you might need from me or anyone else to provide what you need."*

My Strategy Here

Statement	Intent	Heat or Light?
"Harold, the change to new math standards is important to us because it is part of our vision to support our students in better ways. So, the use of new standards is a non-negotiable for all of us. I want to know how you will get started using these standards."	I want to remind Harold of the purpose of the new standards—in hopes that he will see that there *is* a purpose. I also want him to clearly know that all teachers will be basing their instruction on the new standards and that he cannot continue to avoid the use of the standards. The statement that begins with "I want to know how you will get started" is a gentle push to eliminate Harold's inertia to the change.	Heat statements but delivered in a supportive, relationship-rich culture
"But I also want to know how you want to do that and what you might need from me or anyone else to provide what you need."	I want Harold to know that while he must use the standards, *how* he begins using them is his choice. I also want him to feel a sense of genuine support from me and my willingness to provide the support for his action.	Light statements but delivered in a no-nonsense, clear fashion

Resistance Issue: Your Colleagues Really Just Fundamentally Don't Agree With the Change

Strategy: Leverage Some Factors That Will Help Affect His/Her Movement Toward Implementation.

Fullan (2007) describes four factors that work to help alter the resister's beliefs and use of the change. Leaders will want to leverage any or all of these four factors as he or she supports implementation and the elimination of resistance to implementation. In brief, they are

Need. Does the change address a "felt" need with the person? Often, there may be a logical realization that the change is needed, but during implementation, that need may be lost in the day-to-day dilemmas of getting the work done in this new way. The continued perception of need may help the resister remember the overarching purpose of the change, which is, hopefully, one with which he or she can relate.

Clarity. Does the resister clearly understand what he or she is supposed to be doing differently? As the change gets more and more complex, it may become harder and harder for people to describe the essential features of the change.

Complexity. Is the change so large, complex, or extensive that it creates challenges for implementation? Sometimes, the change can seem overwhelming and "too big" for individuals. Or, the change can signal a dramatic change to the individual's practices, and it is easier to resist the change (and take the heat) than embrace the change that seems overwhelming.

Practicality. Does the change have real, easily seen benefits to either the people implementing the change or to their students? If teachers are not sure about the usefulness of the change, they may look at it as "another thing to do."

Again, the leader's response is relatively simple. If it is felt that the person is pushing back because of a fundamental disagreement with the change, I will ask myself the following questions if the answer to any of them is a "no," it perhaps tells me what communication is needed to move the work along.

- Is it possible that this person has lost the "need" or purpose for the change, or we haven't arrived at that mutual purpose that would move him forward?

- Have I been clear on the components of the change and what is different about the change?

- Do I need to consider how to break down the complexity of the change into more manageable parts for folks?

- Are people seeing a payoff to the change? Is there some kind of immediate benefit people will see if they embrace the change?

Strategy: Find the Mutual Purpose That Will Form Our Partnership.

Patterson, Grenny, McMillan, and Switzler (2002) define mutual purpose to "mean that others perceive that we are working toward a common outcome in the conversation, and that we care about their goals, interests, and values. And vice versa. We believe they care about ours" (p. 69). If there is resistance, it can be that the purpose for the change that you believe so deeply in is not shared by the other person. The mutual purpose, then, becomes "the entry point of dialogue" (p. 69) and a catalyst to find a larger goal that we both do hold as important. Our thinking is that the identification of something that we both value will allow us to work together more productively to move the change work forward.

Patterson and his coauthors (2002) identify four steps to a ladder that bring us to this higher ground. These four steps have influenced my ability to achieve a mutual purpose. I'm summarizing my interpretation of their steps in a shortened version:

Get a Mutual Commitment to Seek the Mutual Purpose. This may sound like, "You know, we have talked about this change and I think that part of the issue is that we fundamentally disagree on the purpose for the change. I believe it's going to be hard work but will benefit our students; it seems like you have seen a lot of changes in the past that didn't seem to have a purpose and you wonder if this one will work. So, for now, let's just talk about what we do believe and what we both think is important here at work."

Invent a Mutual Purpose. This may sound like, "So we both want changes and improvements in our instruction but we also don't want to jeopardize a teacher's independence in selecting strategies that work for her students. We also agree that we want the change to not script any teacher's decisions. So, based on that, how do we approach this change and how do you hold true to what we have just identified and yet begin using the new initiative?"

Brainstorm New Strategies. This is just that—the open dialogue about multiple ideas that could both satisfy the mutual purpose and yet adhere to the implementation of the change. If you use this strategy, it is important to keep the idea of brainstorming front and center, not allowing you or the other person to critique the idea as it is suggested. A better plan is to wait until all of the ideas are on the table and then assess each idea according to some criteria that you both agree on.

Remember that the issue with this resister may be that he fundamentally believes the new change is not good either for him or his students. By focusing on the mutual purpose, you and he are afforded a new opportunity to engage in dialogue, and as long as the channels are still open, there is a chance for action that you both can live with.

Strategy: Conduct a "Force Field Analysis" to Help the Person(s) See the Forces Driving Toward the Change and the Forces That Are Resisting the Change.

This strategy puts the change on a shared table for examination. The strategy also acknowledges that difference of opinion but also does not tell the resistant person that the change will go away. Instead, it is a device to examine the forces pressing for the change and the forces working against it—all in an attempt to strengthen the positive forces and eliminate or answer the negative forces. Often, the force field analysis (Kaminski, 2011) is accomplished with the help of a visual diagram much like the representation in Figure 6.3.

When I'm using this strategy with someone, I actually draw a simple graphic on a piece of chart paper (if available) or on my pad of paper to give us a visual to complete. I and the person work to identify lists

Figure 6.3   The Push and Pull of Long-Term Change

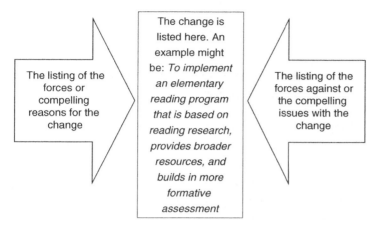

| The listing of the forces or compelling reasons for the change | The change is listed here. An example might be: *To implement an elementary reading program that is based on reading research, provides broader resources, and builds in more formative assessment* | The listing of the forces against or the compelling issues with the change |

of reasons for both sides, and while we explore all of the forces working against the change (including all of his reasons), I am not saying that the change will go away. A force field analysis might seem risky because you are putting all of the "pluses and minuses" on the table, but it really isn't. The act of exploring all of the negative issues or reasons can be a way for the resistant person to look squarely at his or her own logic. Often, when I have used force field analysis, I find that the reasons against the change almost melt away as we are discussing them.

If the issues working against the change still appear formidable, this force field dialogue allows you and the other person to problem solve and improve the probability of the change's success. This strategy offers a balanced way to view the change as you discuss it; your hope is that the analysis will move the person away from his fundamental disagreement with it and clarify the positive aspects of the change.

Resistance Issue: People Start the Change Willingly, but Then Either Lose Interest or Give Up

Strategy: Using the Three Phases of Change, Try to Find Out What the Dilemmas Are.

In the previous chapter, we talked about the kinds of concerns people may have and how those concerns might be preventing them from moving forward with the change. These concerns may range along the following:

Information—wanting to gather information about the change and what is intended as a result of the change

Personal—wondering how the change might affect them personally, whether or not the person thinks he can accomplish the change, or whether or not the change is being viewed as equally demanding on all people expected to implement it

Management—expecting to resolve all of the "task oriented" issues related to the change, such as time management, incorporation of materials, how to maintain classroom control during the new change, and so on

Consequence—concerns about the effects of the change on students, either positive or negative

Identifying the change and then asking what the concerns or dilemmas are is a useful tool, as described in several locations in this book. Odds are that the concerns are almost predictable. Concerns early on, you'll remember, might be more to learn about the innovation or wonder how the change will affect them. Concerns in the middle of the implementation work, though, could move toward more task-focused issues of efficiency. As those concerns are addressed and alleviated, people may then be able to focus on students and whether or not they are benefitting from the change.

The leader's strategy, then, is to ask people what their concerns are (best done individually), and then to match his or her strategy with the concern. See Figure 6.4 for some broad suggestions of matching leader support with the kinds of concerns that might arise during that phase.

Figure 6.4   Addressing the Dilemmas During That Phase of Change

Initiation	Implementation	Institutionalization
Establish the need (the why) for the change	Identify responsibilities for coordination and orchestration	Embed the change within the school structures and operations
Identify a clear approach to the beginning of the change	Apply both heat and light and focus on short-term wins	Eliminate competing priorities or practices
Identify advocates or champions for the change	Broaden champions and informal sharing for management problem solving	Link to other change efforts
Consider how to transfer "top down" to a combination of top down and "bottom up"	Begin shared control over the implementation	Ensure widespread use among entities
Begin user training to establish an acceptable knowledge level	Develop school-based professional learning to support troubleshooting	Develop a bank of internal facilitators
Allocate resources	Adjust resources to include time and targeted support	Measure, assess, and evaluate progress + adjust systems and plans
Develop stratifications of leader awareness and support/build a coalition	Shift leader support to troubleshooting and management issues	

Source: Adapted from Fullan, 2007; Huberman & Miles, 1984; Kotter, 2012; and Tomlinson & Murphy, 2015.

The leader's theory is that the resistant person is not resisting out of sheer intent; rather, he is resisting because at this point in his journey with the change, he needs something and it is not being delivered. I know that in previous sections of this book, I have warned you about solving problems of people too quickly, and here I am advocating it as a way to answer their issues and reduce resistance! So, let me explain. When supporting the change, it is powerful to ask about the concerns and demonstrate *understanding* by not fixing the concern on the spot. Yet, the savvy leader will learn from these conversations; and at some point, will want to share ways to support his colleagues by demonstrating that understanding through appropriate supportive actions. In the case of starting out (initiation) and then losing interest (probably implementation), our job is to find out those roadblocks and then engage the person in conversations whereby the issues are resolved. No matter the intent, our goal is to move the innovation forward and to create a culture of implementation and collaboration. Often, in the right circumstances, the person will resolve them by herself. By finding out the concerns and then working over time to support the resolution of those concerns, the resistance might and probably will fade.

Strategy: Engage in Structured Conversations That Result in a Commitment.

Previously, we looked at the elements of a "bifocal conversation," which not only created the feelings we wanted but also the commitment to a decision (see Figure 6.5).

Figure 6.5   Bifocal Engagement in Partnership Conversations

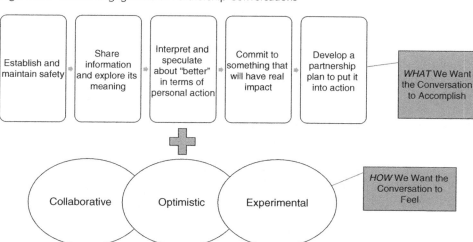

It could be that a simple way to gently move the person who has lost interest back to the work is to make sure that the next few conversations focus more on the last two elements of the top of Figure 6.5. In other words, make sure that your conversations with the person identify something significant in terms of his or her next steps and then conclude with a partnership. This partnership is evidenced by both people stating what they will do. She will state how she will move forward with her next action, and you will state how you will support her through your actions as well.

An Example of the Productive Conversation in Action

Suppose that you have had a good conversation with someone and you have verbalized the work that has already been done by him. You then brainstorm possible next steps with him and ask him to identify one step that he is willing to commit to within a certain amount of time. (Often, at this point in the conversation, you have run out of time and you must go. This is a dangerous place in the conversation to leave, in that it doesn't tie up any loose ends with a contract of sorts between you and him.)

I even like to review at the end, saying something like

> *"Okay, we have really covered a lot of ground today and you have focused on one action that will move you forward [state the action again]. When do you think you will implement that action and how will you communicate with me about it? Also, I want to help. What would be the most useful way for me to support you?"*

Ending the conversation in this way ensures action, because you have both agreed to the terms of it. This is a powerful way to honor the individual and the work that he has already done while holding him to further action. His implementation has only moved him so far, and your non-negotiable is that he will continue to deepen his sophistication of the change.

Strategy: Use the Gradual Release of Responsibility to Rethink Your Support of the Resister(s).

I always wince when I hear of districts that launch a new initiative, plan and hold massive training, and then expect teachers to move right into their classrooms and implement the change independently and sophisticatedly. It just doesn't happen for most folks. Most people doing the work need a cycle of support as they move from timid attempts to independent success.

This idea of providing a cycle of support for the independent use of a skill has been well documented as we work with students. Vygotsky (1980, 1986) described a progression toward independent practice for students as they learn to master new content. I believe the same need for progressive support exists for adults as well as they meet the challenges of a change in their practice. Vygotsky saw this progression as the zone of proximal development and described it as the distance that exists between what people can do independently through personal and individual processing and what that same person can do only with the assistance of a more knowledgeable or skillful peer (Vygotsky, 1980, 1986). Pearson and Gallagher (1983) described the desired progression in terms of the support the person needs in order to be "gradually released" from intensive and regular help. Use Figure 6.6 to study the progression of support and assistance.

The implications here are pretty obvious. We so often haul people in for good training, conducted by competent trainers, where everyone learns about the change. I don't know why we expect people to then magically re-enter their classrooms and feel completely confident with the implementation of this change that they just learned about. Remember that when the change is first initiated, people are often excited about the possibilities of the change and are eager to give it their best shot. However, we sabotage their best intentions by not offering them a pathway to implement the change with gradually releasing support.

Figure 6.6   The Gradual Release of Responsible Change

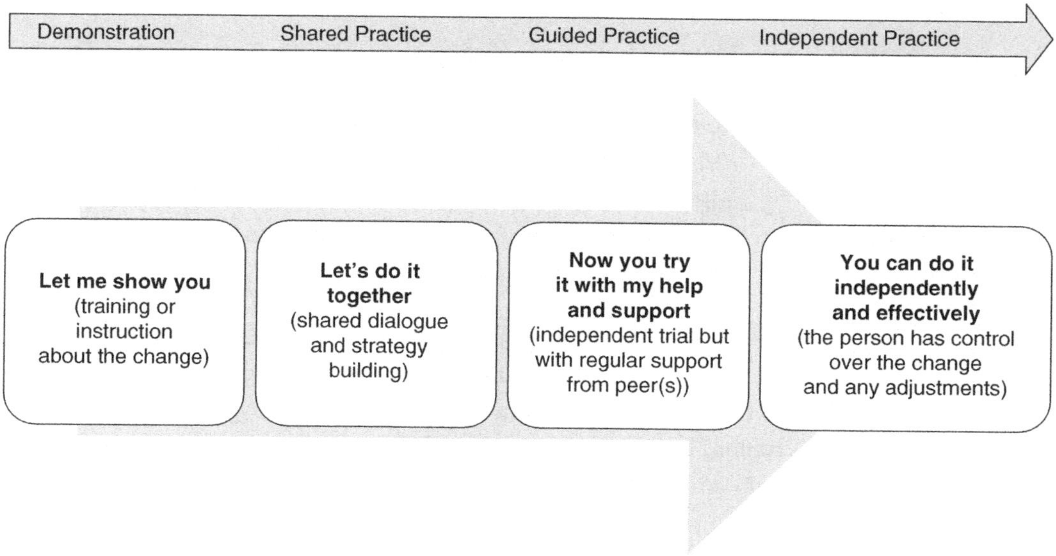

Demonstration   Shared Practice   Guided Practice   Independent Practice

Let me show you
(training or instruction about the change)

Let's do it together
(shared dialogue and strategy building)

Now you try it with my help and support
(independent trial but with regular support from peer(s))

You can do it independently and effectively
(the person has control over the change and any adjustments)

I believe this may be why a lot of people start out strong, and then we find that a few weeks into their work, there are no signs of the implemented change. We simply have asked people to jump too quickly from "let me show you" to "now go do it independently and effectively" without the support they need. The result is resistance, either outwardly or covertly—but in any case, the resistance is an issue and we were complicit in the problem!

Once again, the needed action is clear. When seeing a lot of initial attempts followed by a quick abandonment of the practice, you may want to rethink the kind of school-based support the teachers need to get really proficient in the practice. Implementation is really a school function—and the support that people need must reside at the school. Using the gradual release of responsibility as a reflective piece will help us all reset our support to minimize or reduce the resistance and help us plan better for implementation of the changes we intend to make.

Resistance Issue: The Person(s) Just Seems Irritated by Your Enthusiasm and Focus

Strategy: Apologize.

This simple strategy can be one of your most powerful. Remember that the resistant person has a different point of view about the change and expects you to react in a predictable, defensive way. It may be that your work in the past has caused some uncomfortable feelings between the two of you. Apologizing, and meaning it, may be hard for us. It is, however, a way to "start over" and release the tension. Jennifer Abrams (2009, p. 91) writes an example of an apology that might release the tension between two people. I have adapted it for our use.

> *"Maria, I am sorry for cutting you off in our meeting today. I was frustrated and didn't really allow you to continue with your concerns about the math program. My behavior was belittling. I'm not going to try to explain my reasons. What does matter is that I messed up and I feel badly about my actions toward you. I will try not to get frustrated again and act that way toward you."*

Notice that the apology just focused on my behavior, not hers. That focus is one secret to an effective apology. Apologizing may be hard for us because we may genuinely feel that we had a right to show our frustration, but as Abrams puts it (2009), usually those concerns are about our own comfort, not the comfort of the other person.

Apologizing is asking the other person to "reset" and continue working with you. Often, the sincere apology is that mechanism, as long as the apology isn't derailed by some additional comments from you (Lazare, 2004, as restated by Abrams, 2009) that show your possible insincerity. Note these comments to avoid when apologizing:

- Not owning the apology or identifying your behavior in a vague way

- Making the apology conditional ("If mistakes were made, then I'm sorry.")

- Minimizing the offense

- Implying that the other person might be damaged or weak ("If anyone was hurt" or "If you were offended . . .")

Strategy: Change Your Style of Talking About the Change.

As I've said before, there really is no "most effective way" to have conversations with people about the change you are leading. The conversation's effectiveness depends on an extensive set of variables that include the level of trust between you and the person, the focus and vision, the intent of the conversation, the teacher's degree of knowledge and skill regarding the change, and your degree of knowledge and skill regarding the change.

I propose that in some cases, we can reduce the resistance if we are willing to examine the way we have previously approached the conversation. You will remember in chapter 5 our leadership continuum, Figure 6.7.

Figure 6.7   Leadership Preference Continuum

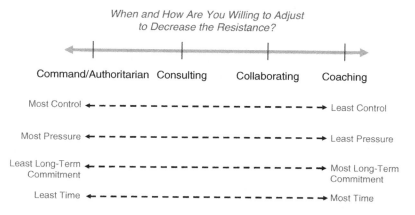

Sometimes, because of our frustration, we adopt (either consciously or unconsciously) more of a command or authoritarian style because we sense the urgency for the work to move forward. In some cases, that style might actually accelerate or deepen the resistance. Leaders may want to "win" the conversation by adopting this style, but it often just compels the resistant person to dig in deeper and fight harder.

This kind of reflection on the way we are delivering the hard conversation is useful to us, as it teaches us to pause before we act and speak and consider the most effective way to engage the person who remains difficult. As I have said before, I often adopted the authoritarian style as a school principal and district leader, simply because that was a comfortable style for me and I sensed the urgency to change. In some cases, that was not the style for my most difficult conversations, and I would have been better served if I had sensed a need to adjust my style to be more collaborative.

The opposite scenario is also true for how we approach these conversations. Sometimes, we approach the resistant person in a more collaborative style, but really what the person might need is a more direct approach (think a bit of respectful heat). In this case, more direction and the gentle assertion to move forward might just be what he or she needs to start implementing the change.

The implications for us as we work with resistant folks are to use this simple continuum to plan our fluidity depending on what the person needs from us. I believe if we have a better "match" between the leader and the person having the conversation, we might be more productive and lessen the need for resistance. We might take a hint from a principal friend and colleague of mine. Sandy simply asks the person how he or she wants her (Sandy) to approach the conversation. After she makes it safe to talk and identifies the topics for conversation (it could be the gap between the expected implementation and what is actually going on), Sandy says something like

> *"So, during the conversation, how do you want me to behave? Would it be helpful if I just gave you my opinion on what you could be doing or are you ready to discuss your own ideas and if so, we could collaborate? Tell me."*

In this way, Sandy is doing what we all should be doing—focusing on results in a relationship-rich way. By asking the person how he or she wants Sandy to handle this conversation, she is communicating respect and partnership. This simple act that Sandy uses all of the time is perhaps her best device to manage resistance and form working partnerships with people. I wish I had been that skilled when I was a principal myself!

Resistance Issue: The Pushback Is Harsh, Vocal, and Aggressive

Strategy: Use the "Gap Conversation" to Break Through the Resistance.

Patterson et al. (2013) describe the gap as a "serious, consequential, and complex deviation, something that might be hard or even risky to discuss" (p. 77). When the resistance is coupled with behaviors that could seriously undermine the change, a *gap conversation* (Patterson et al., 2013) may be in order. Gap conversations focus on accountability and are not intended to damage the relationship between the leader and the person. They are, however, intended to cut through the dialogue and become really clear on expectations for behavior and performance. This combination of heat and light may be just what the person needs to become part of the community implementing the change.

The sequence of a gap conversation varies, but is generally in this order:

1. Create safety by exhibiting respect for the person's effort.

2. Describe the purpose for the conversation and what you hope to achieve.

3. Describe the gap between what is expected and how the person is performing using direct but kind words and tone.

4. Share the impact of the gap—on either students, other teachers, and the school as a whole.

5. Invite the person to explore the gap with you, encouraging frank talk about the lack of implementation to this point.

6. Ask the person to build his or her version of changed behavior that would positively address the gap. Explore it with the person in a nonjudgmental way.

7. Build your own version of his or her changed behavior that would positively address the gap and invite the teacher to explore your version with you.

8. Agree on elements of a plan that can be identified with both versions of changed behavior.

9. Commit to action, set dates, and close the conversation.

The gap conversation is direct and straightforward. It can actually build the relationship with the person, because it holds him or her accountable for action but in a supportive, nonjudgmental way. Patterson and his coauthors (2013) remind us, "Don't play games, merely describe the gap" (p. 81). This transparency has a payoff: you are ensured of action and you have kept the relationship at least the same by managing your own emotion and frustration with the person's lack of movement.

Strategy: Calmly Match Your Response With Your Analysis of the Characteristics of the Resistance.

Remember that this situation is one where the resistance is unusually vocal, harsh, or critical. Usually, in these tough situations, our emotions are very much in play. I find that thinking about my behavior in these tough moments is useful to me. There are always options for us, we should remember. Adam Kahane (2017) found that when we face situations of problems or resistance, we generally have four ways to behave or respond. I have learned much from his point of view and have adapted his "four ways to respond" to address resistance. These adapted four ways are represented in Figure 6.8.

Figure 6.8   Analyzing the Leader's Response

Source: Kahane, 2017.

Yes, I can live with the resistance situation because it has limited impact or it cannot be changed in this circumstance. There are essentially two ways to rationally respond if you determine that you can live with the resistant behavior or that the resistant behavior is developmental and you are fairly sure that it will subside on its own or because of other factors.

- We can *adapt* when we think that we cannot change the situation and do not need to. Therefore, the work will be to figure out a way to live with it. "Adapting may require us to employ lots of intelligence and ingenuity and courage, but we do this within a limited sphere. We believe that we are not able to change what is happening outside our immediate area of influence; we cannot change the rules of the game, so we must play it as well as we can" (Kahane, 2017, p. 21). Adapting also means that we do not expend a large amount of energy on the resistant behavior; in fact, you believe that if you devote a lot of your energy and resources to the behavior that is exceptional—the behavior of the people who are implementing the change at high levels and achieving their goals—then the resistant behavior might change because of how the time, communication, and resources are being distributed.

- We may *exit* when we believe that we cannot change the behavior and we are no longer willing to deal with it. Exiting is quitting or walking away. I liken it to ignoring the resistant behavior—it just doesn't exist for you or it is something that you can handle by omission. For most of us, exiting is not an option, in that when the resistant behavior is hurting our school, the students, or other adults, it demands a response.

No, I can't live with the current resistance situation and it can be changed. There are generally two ways to behave and respond if you determine that the resistance must be faced and remedied.

- You *collaborate* if you believe that the resistance can be positively affected and that the best way to do it is to collaborate with that person or persons. Our firm belief is that the best solution will be found in the sharing of ideas, understanding of points of view, and determination to jointly work toward the mutual purpose. Collaborating takes time, and in some cases, it takes too much time if the resistant behavior needs an immediate reversal.

- You *force* if you think that you, alone, have the best information to determine what must be done. You feel a responsibility to impose that change in behavior on the other person and hopefully can decide on a method that is peaceful and not defeating to the other person. A danger in forcing is that sometimes your forceful behavior signals "what you think should be done, and others who think differently will push back, and therefore we will not achieve the outcome we intend" (Kahane, 2017, p. 21).

This strategy of "Can I live with it?" reminds us that there are a range of responses from us to the resistant behavior; in some instances, collaboration is not the answer. Equally important to remember is that forcing is not always the answer, either. Taking a few moments to think about the most impactful response from you is one key to working through the resistance and not inadvertently making it even more formidable.

When reading through the five kinds of resistance issues and the 12 viable, reliable strategies to deal with the issues, I'm reminded of the complexity of the nature of this beast. Resistance can be confusing, disheartening, and sometimes debilitating. It can also signal a moment when we can learn from the pushback in order to make the change even stronger and more lasting. For me, the secret to dealing with resistant folks is not to react but take the time to consider the circumstances, my goals, the nature of the change, and what I would like the relationship with the person to signal. As for the 12 strategies, I only ask you to try some of them out. Match the most likely strategy with the issue and give it your best effort. More times than not, you will be pleasantly surprised by the reaction.

CHAPTER 7

PRODUCTIVE TALK ABOUT THE CHANGE

Develop a partnership of dialogue, respect, and action.

KEY PRACTICE

Effective Conversations Are Your Most Powerful Tools for Learning and Change

A few years ago, I was asked to work in a middle school just south of a large metropolitan area in Texas. Ten of the teachers had volunteered to invite me into their classrooms for four visits each and engage with me in individual coaching conversations. I'll never forget one experience I had with a social studies teacher who had just a few years of experience. She taught me a valuable lesson about the power of the conversation.

After my second visit to her classroom, I sat down with her for what I thought would be a great conversation. I was committed to a coaching conversation format—one that demonstrated collaboration, facilitation, and probing questions. When we sat down for that conversation, I was ready. After I created a sense of safety with her and we talked about the purpose of the conversation, I began peppering her with (in my opinion) great questions. She began answering me haltingly, and just a couple of minutes into the talk I felt that the conversation was getting a bit awkward. She must have had the same feeling, because at about that same moment she leaned over in my direction and put her hand on my arm. She said, "Mike, will you stop for a minute?" Trying to be mindful of her emotions and her reasons for halting the talk, I asked her to tell me what wasn't working for her. She quickly answered, "You keep asking me questions about what I would do differently. I don't know. I'm waiting for *you* to tell me what you would do. I need *your* ideas."

I will never forget that teacher, because she helped me remember that a valuable conversation is based in part on *what the person needs*, not what I think. This teacher was working as hard as she could, and yet she didn't feel successful. Relying on her own ideas was futile because she had already explored those and still wasn't satisfied. She needed a certain approach from me, and I wasn't delivering it. There was a mismatch in terms of how I was going about the conversation, and if I didn't correct it immediately, the teacher would probably think that this had been a waste of time for her.

> I also believe that conversations, designed and conducted in a way that maintain a laser-like focus on the purpose and goal while reinforcing the relationship, are keys to minimizing the possibility of resistance or reducing the resistance that has already appeared.

This conversation had started out badly, but with her help, I was able to alter my approach so we could learn and understand her teaching—together. Leaders frequently have these kinds of conversations with teachers, and I wonder if we sometimes engage in these talks "because we are supposed to" and not because they are perhaps the most valuable tool we have to not only (a) lead the change, but also (b) learn from the teacher about her current practice and (c) assess the progress he or she is making toward full institutionalization of the change (Tomlinson & Murphy, 2015).

I also believe that conversations, designed and conducted in a way that maintain a laser-like focus on the purpose and goal while reinforcing the relationship, are keys to minimizing the possibility of resistance or reducing the resistance that has already appeared. I worry that we are beginning to feel these conversations as "required" in our current leadership challenges. The feeling of requirement can mean that we accomplish the conversations as a way to "check off" this requirement. If we think that, we are abusing a powerful tool for leading and managing the change over time.

Avoid the Common Pitfalls of
Unproductive Conversations

It's likely that many teachers often think of their conversations with us like an exercise in both intellectual and emotional ambush. Teachers often feel that they are approaching such conversations as unequal participants, because it is usually the leader who schedules the time, sets the agenda, and determines the purpose. These kinds of typical conversations do little to form a partnership with teachers or build the relationship for long-term improvement. In fact, in conversations where the leader is completely in control, the teacher usually sits and behaves in a way that he thinks is expected of him rather than engaging in a balanced exchange of ideas and points of view.

This typical kind of conversation about the change is heavily influenced by an encouragement to "wrong spot" (Stone & Heen, 2014). In this scenario, we have a few minutes and feel that we are obligated to point out a better practice, believing our job is to spot the "wrong" and identify "better" for the person. The race to accountability that has swept the country for years may be partially to blame; in addition, many teacher evaluation systems rely on the leader identifying an "area of improvement" for the teacher. I view the selection of what the teacher needs to improve as ineffective, as I'm pretty sure that one-sided improvement conversation will result in short-term changes at best. In fact, we often legitimately want to point out an area of practice that can be improved, and yet the teacher may hear it quite differently than intended.

Quite often, leaders give feedback, and the way we provide it can trigger a variety of unproductive responses. Stone and Heen (2014) list three:

- **Truth Triggers** are simply statements or information we give that aren't true or at best, are somehow "off." There was honest intent to give information that is useful; however, because it isn't the reality that the teacher sees, he can feel indignant, wronged, or just exasperated at our lack of understanding.

- **Relationship Triggers** are based on how the teacher feels he is being treated or the perception that we are intentionally demeaning or that because of the fragility of the relationship between us, we are sending a negative message about what we believe about the teacher.

- **Identity Triggers** are when the person believes that the conversation between the leader and her will cause "her identity to come undone" (p. 17). The person then feels overwhelmed, threatened, ashamed, or just off balance, not sure what to think of him- or herself anymore.

The problem with these triggers is that they are perceived as legitimate by the person and they keep us from engaging in a productive conversation with that person. Stone and Heen (2014) remind us that these conversations should instead be ones which involve "learning how the other person sees things; of trying on ideas that at first seem like a poor fit; of experimenting" (p. 17).

Create Conversations About the Change in a Way That Demonstrate the Long-Term Partnership

We can all probably agree to try to avoid the conversation pitfalls that we just described. The question, then, is "how can we design and conduct conversations that both focus on the results and build the partnership?" Charlotte Danielson (2009) shares insights at the very beginning of her book *Talk About Teaching*. "What is important is that the conversation is enhanced by the skill of those conducting it to dig below the surface, to help teachers examine underlying assumptions and likely consequences of different approaches," she writes (p. 1). I believe Danielson has accurately captured our purpose for these conversations. We want the talks with our teachers to dig below the surface and challenge *both* the teacher's and *our* points of view about what would work better for students. You will remember from our previous work that no matter where we are in the change journey, we will also want these conversations to identify small "wins" to encourage the teacher to acknowledge his or her growth and look forward to additional efforts.

Thus, the most effective conversations about the change will be characterized by cycles of information sharing, thinking, brainstorming, acting, and interpreting. A central belief of mine is that the conversation can do it all—reinforce the relationship between me and the teacher and focus on the changes that must take place to achieve even better results with students. Figure 5.4 in chapter 5 identifies the productive conversation, particularly with the resistant person. I believe that the same foundation is most effective and supportive with *any* person who is sharing his or her work and progress with me. In chapter 6, Figure 6.5 expanded the same figure first seen in Figure 5.4, detailing not only the "how we want the conversation to feel" but also "what I want the conversation to accomplish. While the *what* identifies five steps or fundamental guideposts and they seem to follow a logical sequence, we should not assume that all great conversations will follow that sequence in a predictable, lockstep manner. Here is the expanded version of the components of partnership conversations in Figure 7.1.

Figure 7.1   Bifocal Engagement in Partnership Conversations

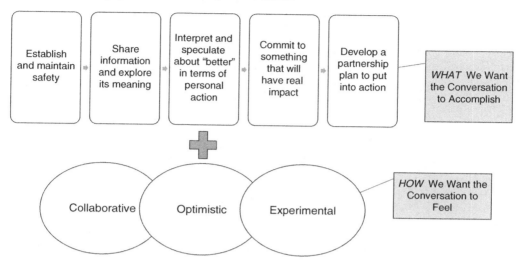

The *What*

Establish and maintain safety is the art of beginning the conversation well and maintaining a productive tone throughout it. Simply put, the creation of safety is paying attention to the conditions that will make it okay for the person to talk about the work with you. Lots of people establish safety by engaging in small talk with the person. Small talk certainly has its place. "It's a way of reconnecting and engaging with a person, of building relationships, or remembering that other people are human and reminding them that you are human too" (Stanier, 2016, p. 37). Patterson et al. (2013) encourage leaders not to play games with the person, however, by "circling the issue" or engaging in small talk that is completely unrelated to the topic. Safety is established by clearly describing the purpose of the conversation while conveying a sense of caring and understanding. Note that establishing safety is critical at the beginning of the conversation. Equally important is for the leader to notice when safety is in danger or is being breached during the conversation.

Share information and explore its meaning moves the conversation to the exchange of information that has led to this conversation. I find that at this point in the conversation, if safety has been established, I can pretty easily move to the purpose of the conversation and the information that I believe I have that has brought me to want to have this talk with the person. Important is the *exchange* of information, not just the leader sharing his or her perspective and assuming that perspective is accurate. So, I will also encourage the person to share information he has and use that to help both of us build a complete understanding.

Interpret and speculate about "better" in terms of personal action requires both the leader and the person to gather meaning from the information they have shared with each other, leading to speculation about what "better" or the next steps might be for both the leader and the person. Often, I will ask the person to "make sense of what we have been saying" or "put our talk so far in your own words. What are we saying here?" as a way to move the conversation forward. I also believe that if we are building a partnership intended to move us forward, I need to make a commitment to my own action that might move us both forward.

Commit to something that will have real impact is the moment when we are making the golden turn, moving from discussion and idea generation to the selection of some actions (on both of our parts) that will deepen our interdependent relationship and enhance our practices. Depending on the phase of change we are in (or the phase that the teacher is in), I will sometimes identify the possible actions we have brainstormed and then ask, "Which of these would you be willing to take on? Which of these would make the most difference in your classroom?" In keeping with our partnership and my own responsibilities in this effort, I will also ask, "Of the ideas I have thought about that might support you and our change, which of them would you advise me to take on?"

Develop a partnership to put into action is the time for summarizing the conversation and seriously thinking about the next steps. Often, the entire conversation has gone quickly and needs a pause for both the leader and the person to reflect on the topics covered and the commitments made. If this is the case, another brief meeting may need to be scheduled to review the ideas and decide which ones will be put into action. Patterson et al. (2013) also reminds us that the summary should ask the person's input for issues that might need mentioning. In essence, this is the point in the conversation when you are talking about moving forward with the improvement. Therefore, specific actions, timelines, and dates for follow-up should be examined.

The *What* Combined With the *How*

Many conversations will not exactly follow this five-part sequence, but it helps the leader to plan as if the conversation will. The *what* of the conversation identifies the products of the conversation—the information and the committed actions for improvement. The *how* of the conversation is how we want the conversation to feel for the other person. I want the conversation to feel *collaborative*, and so I'll plan to ensure that the other person talks as much as I and shares as much information as I have. I'll also want to assume positive intentions and portray a sense of *optimistic* accomplishment; therefore, I will approach the person as though they are going to be as committed to the action as I will. I also want to establish a tone of *experimentation*, so I will not be too quick to judge or "land" on an action that I think will make the practice better. Look back in chapter 5 for descriptions of those three adjectives that capture the culture or atmosphere of the conversation that is as equally important as the *what*.

The conditions of optimism and experimentation are important foundational principles, because part of your communication to the person will be that you think he or she can develop the skills or capabilities to achieve even more. Dweck (2006) identifies "fixed versus growth assumptions" as critical to the success of adult and student achievement. If a person carries a fixed mindset with them at work, then he or she believes that their capabilities are limited and that when meeting a challenge, they may not have "what it takes" to achieve. By contrast, a person with a growth mindset assumes that the challenge identified in the conversation can be achieved with focused, additional effort (Dweck, 2006).

I think Dweck would also agree with me that often, as leaders, we approach people as though we already think we know what they are capable of—and that assumption drives and alters our relationship with them. Think of the times we have identified a person as "a great teacher" or "a great thinker," and in those simple words, have categorized people in terms of something we believe they were born with. The conversation that I have described in Figure 7.1 submits the alternate way of thinking—that all people with whom we work are capable and eager to do their best and to achieve more and more.

Jump Feet First Into Dialogue

If these important conversations are to feel optimistic, experimental, and collaborative, the leader must design them with a partnership point of view. Central to the success, then, is also how the leader conducts the conversation. Partnership is supported by dialogue, and it is the effective leader's intent to approach the majority of his or her conversations with both of these goals—to showcase a collaborative partnership with the teacher and to engage in the conversation in terms of dialogue.

Patterson et al. (2002) describe dialogue as simply the "free flow of meaning between two or more people." They remind us that both the leader and the teacher approach these conversations with goals, feelings, opinions, theories, and experiences. "This unique combination of thoughts and feelings makes up our personal pool of meaning. This pool not only informs us but also propels our every action" (p. 21). Our aim in having these conversations is that we will not share "my pool" versus "your pool"; instead, the effective leader creates a "pool of shared meaning." The skilled leader, the authors (2002) remind us, does his or her best to make it safe for each person to add their personal meaning to the shared pool.

This is a useful analogy, for it reminds us that the point is not to "win" or to create circumstances where the other person accepts our point of view. Rather, the purpose is for both of us to learn about our response to the anticipated change while staying clear on the purpose of the change. If we hope that these conversations spark a discovery and interpretation of the teacher's current practices along with decisions of how to improve those practices, we must approach the conversation in a way that simultaneously reinforces the purpose and the results we are seeking as well as the importance of the teacher's effort and our support of that effort. There are a few guidelines that help us get really clear on our intent for the conversation and how to work toward dialogue (Tomlinson & Murphy, 2015). See Figure 7.2.

The bottom line is that we may have to adjust our own mindsets in order to approach these conversations in this manner. Instead of using the time as a way to deliver information, it's probably a good idea to think of these conversations as a way to learn about the teacher's practices while guiding collaborative decisions for improvement. Jim Knight (2011) offers another condition necessary to the kinds of conversations we must have about the changes in our schools: "Real communication is a two-way process, and for it to be authentic and humane, we need to take in at least as much as we put out. To be good communicators, we need to be good listeners" (p. 211).

Knight's words "authentic and humane" really strike me, for they ask us to change our normal pattern of encouraging change.

Figure 7.2   Broad Guidelines for Dialogue

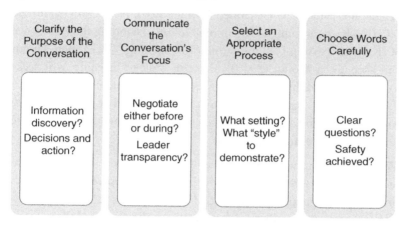

Clearly identified in his comments are the ideas that our conversations must be two-way and empathetic, demonstrating "a need to both understand a person's condition from their perspective and understand the needs of others, with the aim of acting to make a difference in responding to those needs" (Tomlinson & Murphy, 2018, p. 21). This leadership frame of thinking may confront many leaders; so, before I lose you altogether, let me offer the following. The kinds of conversations we have been having have not been collaborative; at best, they have been to offer feedback. These typical conversations have not generally worked or built trust. Instead of repeating the same manner over and over, is it time to be bold and change our approach? I firmly believe that people are giving us the best they have, and I trust them to work with me on common purposes. If you agree with me, then perhaps we are all ready to take the plunge into the common pools of meaning with our folks.

Listen to Learn and Understand

If we are to find this common pool of meaning with the folks we lead, it seems that the act of listening is the most means to learn what that common pool of meaning might be. Listening is how we can demonstrate that spirit of collaboration and curiosity. Just as important is the power of listening to learn from the other person. It is through that joint learning that we can discover what we have in common and what will hold us together as we proceed into the change in a more sophisticated way. To put it simply, this is the kind of listening that "values listening in its own right, not as a stepping stone to something else" (Tschannen-Moran & Tschannen-Moran, 2010, p. 69). These authors (2010) refer to listening as intentional in understanding the experience of the other person. Calling it "mindful listening," Tschannen-Moran and Tschannen-Moran (2010) value this kind of listening as it seeks to appreciate a different point of view. Mindful listening is crucial to the leader of change, for much of the resistance that he or she may encounter may be due to that different point of view that leads to the implementor's confusing behavior.

Mindful listening requires us to be well aware of "the running stream of thoughts and feelings you (we) have during the conversation in reaction to what's going on" (Stone & Heen, 2014, p. 234). These running streams of thoughts and feelings we are having can be our worst enemies, for they create strong internal barriers to understanding and learning. Stone and Heen (2014) warn that these "inside editors of what is being said" are often fairly quiet; but when we disagree with what is being said or begin to feel emotional, our internal editing voice becomes overpowering and begins to demand so much of our attention that the voice of the other person is softened or even silenced.

I often find that my internal distractions, the voice that I hear more than the other person's, is more potent than the external distractions I may feel or sense. And perhaps like you, I have to really pay attention to monitoring that internal voice. More than likely, all of us were originally recognized for our leadership potential because we were intuitive and could evaluate a situation quickly. Those skills, while highly regarded in the leadership world, may actually be some of our worst enemies when we are listening to someone. It's hard for me not to quickly size up what is being said and suspend that judgment to learn. In addition, while our quick intuition is certainly prized, we can also be seduced into thinking that our intuition is usually right. There are many cases when it is possible that the other person is bringing a valuable point of view to the conversation about change in your school. Being aware of how our internal voices can cloud that point of view is the first step to being a more productive, mindful listener.

While every conversation is different and there is no recipe for mindful listening, there are some conditions and concepts that help us all be better at it. Tschannen-Moran & Tschannen-Moran (2010) and Cheliotes and Reilly (2010) align to describe five of these concepts that help remind us of an efficient and effective, relationship-focused conversation. Figure 7.3 illustrates those reminders. Reflect on and evaluate your expertise in each.

Figure 7.3   Five Aspects of Mindful Listening

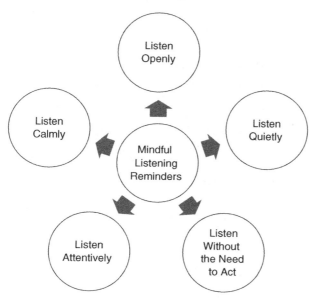

- **Listen openly.** How well do you suspend your own personal judgment about what is being said? Is it easy for you to demonstrate genuine curiosity about the other person's ideas?

- **Listen quietly.** Are you comfortable with being silent? Or, do you find yourself dominating the conversation without even trying?

- **Listen without the need to act.** Do you sometimes jump in and own the problem or own the solution without drawing out the teacher's thinking?

- **Listen attentively.** How well can you limit the internal and external distractions while you are conversing?

- **Listen calmly.** How clear can you remain to the purpose of the conversation and not get emotionally sidetracked by things that are said?

I often talk about the difference between reacting and responding to the person with whom I'm talking. Reacting, to me, is just that—a bit of a quick, hastily created set of words from me that is developed and uttered quickly. Reactions are tough—they usually communicate emotion just as much as they communicate understanding. Because of the crunch

Perfectly
productive
conversations
may be derailed
by our quick
reactions.

of time, we are often pushed into resolving a conversation quickly and may be compelled to react quickly to what is said in order for us to move forward. Those are dangerous circumstances. Perfectly productive conversations may be derailed by our quick reactions. I always try to remember that between me and the other person, I probably have a little more perceived power than the other. Reactions, in my opinion, abuse that power and develop an imbalanced exchange of ideas.

On the other hand, responding removes the carelessness from our words. Responding means that we are taking the time to consider our words before they leave our mouths. Again, Knight (2011) asks us to think about two behaviors in responding: (1) authentically think about what has been said and (2) consider our words and their effect before we speak. I find that I may need even more time than I have during that conversation to make sure I understand what is being said. Think about it: Sometimes, if we are in the middle of this crucial conversation, the best thing that might occur is for you to say something like, "This has been important and you have said a lot that I want to consider. I'd like to take a day to make sure I reflect on this. Can we get together tomorrow to continue?" I call this "making a date," and it signals several important messages to the other person. First, it says that what he or she has been saying is valuable to you. Second, it communicates that you want to carefully consider the meaning. Third, it gives us both a "pause" so we can respond appropriately instead of reacting.

Use Effective Questions to "Drill Down" Into the Meaning

If mindful listening is the key to learning and understanding another's point of view, then skillful questioning must be the device to guide the time we must take to learn and understand. "Quality questions are authentic; they might be posed to gain specific information, to understand another's point of view, to help others make personal meaning, to stimulate reflection and self-awareness, and to solve problems" (Walsh & Sattes, 2010, p. 12). As Walsh and Sattes remind us, there is no such thing as a perfect question. But they are powerful means to get at the heart of the issue or subject. Yet, questioning takes careful time to prepare and to deliver— many leaders would like to "go about their daily affairs without questioning everything" (Berger, 2014, p. 6). I find, however, that when our conversations with people are embedded with thoughtful questions, we both learn more and are pushed to dig deeper than perhaps we would have.

Questions have the ability to gently force us to confront our assumptions and ways of thinking and believing. In the change process, all of us are constantly trying to make sense of the change and how it is affecting both us and our stakeholders; and when our "change conversations" use questions, it is more probable that one or each of us feels a feeling of discovery and new learning (Berger, 2014).

Words are important for communication accuracy, but words are also important because—if they are worded carefully and empathetically—"they also communicate information about the relationship between the speaker and the listener" (Walsh & Sattes, 2010, p. 17). Thoughtfully worded questions can provide that "pressure and support," a simultaneous urging for the person to examine his or her work more deeply—while also demonstrating that these probes can also gently build the relationship.

So, what is a good question? As said before, there is no perfect formula for great questions—because they live within a context of your purpose. See Figure 7.4.

Clarity of the purpose leads us to design the most effective question. As suggested in Figure 7.4, there are two goals for us as we frame the great questions—to examine *what* I want to focus on and also to carefully plan *how* to lead into it. As Walsh and Sattes (2010) remind us, sometimes the topic that we select is strategic because it will lead us into the real cause or issue. Therefore, wording questions carefully is critical, and their effect (the *how*) is also paramount. We have to "be sure that the questions you will pose are clear in content and convey the intended tone—one that has been chosen with the person who will answer them" (Tomlinson & Murphy, 2015). I have said that there is

Figure 7.4   Do I Ask or Tell?

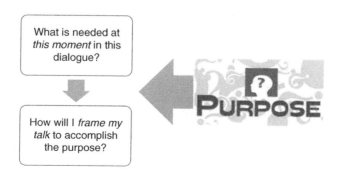

no perfect question—it depends on what I want to talk about and how I want it to feel for both of us—and yet we sometimes get more creative with our questions because we see some examples that might work for us (with our own personal modifications). See Figure 7.5 for some examples of questions I use.

Perhaps these examples may spark some creativity on your part to think more strategically about the questions we ask. Remember that asking good questions is only beneficial if they accomplish your purpose and

Figure 7.5   Samples of Partnership Questions

#1 Questions to Elevate Positive Energy and Confidence	#2 Questions to Focus on What Is Going Well
• What was the most successful part of your lesson?	• What was the best part of the experience for you?
• What personal talents and attributes did you incorporate into your work?	• What was the best part of the classroom experience for the students?
• In what ways does this work reflect the kind of community we live in?	• How do you feel about the assessment strategies you used in the lesson?
• How do you feel the lesson progressed as it went on?	• How did you meet the needs of the varieties of people with whom you work?
• How did you keep the students engaged throughout the lesson?	• How do you feel the lesson linked to the students' prior knowledge?
• What is pleasing you the most about this work?	• What did you learn from implementing the work?
• How did the positive environment in the classroom help the lesson?	• How do you feel the students progressed toward their learning goals?
• What strategies did you use to maintain the motivation and meet the needs of the students?	
#3 Questions to Examine the Person's Desire to Get Better	#4 Questions to Encourage Planning and Tangible Steps
• What would you want to do differently the next time you do this?	• Which of your aspirations are you going to work on?
• What expectations do you have for your students at the end of this year in this skill? What are the implications for how you teach it?	• Which of your strengths do you think best relates to your aspirations?
	• What are your concerns about trying something new? How can I help with that?

- Are there students that you are concerned about? If so, what are some different strategies you might use to help these struggling students?
- What might be your next step as you go deeper in this skill?
- How can this skill be more deeply connected to student experience or the real world?
- What is your evidence today that the work is having an impact? What would be the next step for you?
- What are some other possibilities you might use next time to incorporate more assessment?
- What are you still not satisfied with? How would you measure your success in that area?
- Where do you want to be by the next time I visit your classroom? What do you want changed?

- Which of the new strategies we've discussed do you think would be the most successful?
- How do you feel your work will evolve now?
- Which of the strategies would be the most fun to try?
- Which of the strategies are you willing to try?
- Which strategy would make the most difference to your most diverse students?

convey the feeling you want. Time and time again, I have emphasized the idea that long-term change is not a journey for the leaders of quick fixes. Great conversations with people doing the work are critical if we are to help people remain focused and be honored for their efforts. Jim Knight (2011) summarizes good overall questioning strategies:

Be Curious: The real purpose of questions is to convey something that we truly want to explore and authentically want to hear the point of view the person has. "Curiosity is the embodiment of the principle of reciprocity. When we view conversations as reciprocal, we enter into conversations as learners not talkers. When we are curious, we see a conversation as a living interaction that we co-construct with our partner" (Knight, 2011, p. 213).

Ask Open-Ended, Opinion Questions: We all know that closed questions really target a limited, expected response. Open-ended questions, by contrast, convey several messages: (a) "I value your idea or opinion" and (b) "I am very willing to alter my point of view after I learn from you." Both messages are uplifting and pertinent to the long-term work.

Be Nonjudgmental: Michael Fullan (2008) writes of the importance of leaders holding onto the focus and the vision of the work. And yet, he warns that we have to "hold a strong moral position without succumbing to moral superiority as [your] sole change strategy (p. 60). It may be hard to do, but listening and learning with positive presumptions and without drawing quick conclusions may need to be part of the conversation in our heads when engaging in these critical moments with people.

So, what happens when these conversations do not go as well as you intended? There may be a multitude of reasons we perceive our conversations to be less than effective. Here are a few:

Was I clear on the purpose and was that the other person's purpose? Sometimes, the problem may be that you were clearer on your purpose, but yours didn't match the other person's. In other words, the person may have entered into the conversation with another need entirely in mind; when the conversation takes a turn toward your destination, the person could become defensive or just interpret the dialogue as a way for you to get to *your* destination.

Did I spend too much time thinking about my next question and not enough time on hearing and understanding? If you are like me, you really try to craft the best questions possible and then try to remember them when you are in the moment! Sometimes I'm successful and sometimes not. I wonder if we are frequently so focused on our next question that we forget to hear what is in front of us.

Should I have scrapped my plan and simply heard and understood? We know how important purpose is to the quality conversation. If our purpose obviously isn't the other person's, it seems logical that at times we should abandon our plan and simply go with what the other person is conveying. Often the other person's priority is simply to be heard. Conveying understanding of what is being said can go a long way in building trust with the person; in addition, showing that understanding may be a pathway for *our learning* about the change and how it is going.

At the beginning of this chapter, I suggested that the productive conversation may be our most powerful tool in both leading and managing the change you are seeking. I don't have to remind you that our goal is long-term, impactful improvement in the knowledge and skills of teachers so the students will prosper. Leading the change requires us to get focused on our purpose and vision along with putting into place plans based on the initiation, implementation, and institutionalization of the innovation. Managing the change may indeed be the day-to-day conversations that tell us what is inside the minds of the people doing the innovative work and how they are feeling about it. Leading without learning from these conversations is fruitless; leading with learning from these conversations is both uplifting and meaningful, delivering information and understandings that might be concealed otherwise.

Take a Moment

In thinking about the way I handle my conversations with people, to what extent do I

- understand my own emotions that I often feel when I conduct the conversations;

- carefully plan my conversations;

- conduct my conversations to build optimism, experimentation, and collaboration;

- suspend my need to convey meaning to my need to understand his or her meaning;

- practice the five elements of mindful listening;

- ask effective questions;

- adjust my preferred leadership style to better match my approach to what people are needing during the conversations;

- consider timing, the stakes, and options before having the conversation;

- think about not only what I want to say to the person but also how I want both of us to feel during the conversation; and

- make sure that all of my tough conversations reinforce the results that we are trying to achieve and the relationships that we are building?

OUR TWO SCHOOL DISTRICTS AND THEIR ATTEMPTS TO HAVE PRODUCTIVE TALK ABOUT THE CHANGE

Having continuous conversations about the change—which demonstrate listening and a partnership among the change agents—is critical to the success of any change at schools. Our communication goal in leading change is to develop the "free flow of meaning between people" (Patterson et al., 2002), which can both propel the change and provide a clear lane for the change to follow. Our two districts developed patterns of communication during the initiation and implementation of their respective changes. As we will see in our two districts, effective large-scale communication to support the change doesn't happen accidentally. It is the result of careful planning, the careful crafting of language, a focus on the goal, and consistency across leaders.

Kingsport City Schools

Kingsport leaders were determined to fulfill the promise of a new kind of instructional coach in their schools, and they had some successes and some missteps in their communication. We will analyze their communication in terms of how the change was led, how they dealt with role confusion, and in what ways they responded to problems.

The change to the new role of the InDeS was led by their director in a rather dominant, authoritarian way. This is no criticism, because the approach was not without reason. There was a history of negative perceptions with the former version of school-based instructional coaches. The director was determined that, in this case, the new instructional coach would not be viewed as similar to the old version. For this reason, he forced a name change for the coaching role early on and began to require that this new name be used by all district personnel. He also communicated to district leaders that he didn't want the new version to be driven by former rationale for instructional coaches, which was that instructional coaches did their most impactful work with *only* the most deficient teachers. The new version of instructional coaching was to be guided by the idea that all teachers could benefit from coaching and that coaching works best when built on existing strengths, not weaknesses.

This "command" way of leading change may not always be our preferred style; but at this moment, for what he wanted to accomplish, the command or authoritarian approach was probably the most appropriate for our director. Our study of the leadership style continuum has reminded us that this style may be the most effective if the change must be clear and distinct from the former and if the leader has all of the information he or she needs to direct the transition. This was the case for Kingsport—the director felt that a clear break from the old instructional coaching version was necessary. He wanted the comparison between new and old coach to be like "night and day," and he was loathe to allow much variation in that comparison.

One of the things that drives effective change is clarity—and the director certainly provided that. His leadership of the InDeS provided some comfort to other school leaders in that critical attributes of the new version were emphatically communicated to them. Even the new director, who came to the district in the third year of this implementation, also chose *not* to change much of the way the InDeS were being used. This consistency in communication from the former to the new director of schools provided the kind of continuity that people were seeking and supported the continued implementation of the initiative without a hiccup.

One of the communication issues, however, appeared early on and dogged the initiative for quite a while. This was confusion about the InDeS role as interpreted by the InDeS and the InDeS' principals. Ashley Carter, an original InDeS, explains: "I walked into that role (at that school) and there was some confusion as to how I was to serve—I wasn't supposed to serve as an interventionist and work with kids; there was some conflict with the administrator at first and her vision versus what the district wanted my role to be. She would ask me to do certain things—such as sit in on all collaboratives, and she pushed me to work with teachers in the most need." Her principal requests were not in line with the director's vision of the InDeS, and this same kind of confusion between InDeS and principal did not just occur with Carter. Several other InDeS described their frustration with the same issues. This general topic was a frequent item of conversation in InDeS meetings that first year and part of the second.

Carter not only described the nature of the communication role confusion; in hindsight, she also identified probably the best strategy if there could have been a "do over" in communicating the InDeS role: "I wonder how it might have gone differently if we had some meetings with InDeS and principals together, early on. My understanding was that the InDeS came about because the principals had asked for it. But maybe they thought that because they had asked for it, they could use us any way they could. This may have contributed to some confusion."

(Continued)

(Continued)

Role confusion may have contributed to the reluctance some principals had in developing their contracts with their InDeS. The role confusion certainly was a part of the slight disconnect district leaders observed in how the principals viewed instructional help and how InDeS viewed instructional help. Once again, the district response to this role confusion issue was to put it on the table and address it over and over, pressing for conformity while acknowledging different points of view. Gradually, over time, because of their consistent language, the role confusion dissolved.

The Kingsport leaders, as said many times before, were not afraid to examine communication issues closely. Their refusal to sweep problems under the table worked well for them. For instance, district leaders made it very clear that they were always available for dialogue with individual InDeS or principals during the transition to this new form of instructional coach. "I also not only spent time on site with the principals and coaches, I also engaged in virtual training and phone conversations with primarily coaches to handle individual implementation issues that were coming up," Stephanie Potter, the leader (during the first three years) of the InDeS explains. "I made myself available to principals too and a few contacted me multiple times for phone conversations."

The Kingsport City Schools leaders were focused on their new definition of instructional coaching and were determined to make it happen. They achieved widespread success in their implementation of the InDeS, based on results from students, teachers, and principals. Key illustrations of how Kingsport leaders managed their communication of the initiative include the following:

- The director assumed a particular leadership style at first which took control of the instructional coaching perceptions and outlined a new view of coaching.

- District leaders made "command" decisions that quickly changed the name of the coach but also clearly defined the mindset change regarding the new version.

- They realized that they had moved into implementation with only moderate understanding of the particulars of the InDeS role. When faced with role confusion, they spent hours with both InDeS and principals, clarifying the roles and coming to consensus.

- The new director chose not to change many aspects of InDeS functions when he assumed the role in the third year of implementation.

- District leaders made themselves available to both InDeS and principals at all times and engaged in many one-on-one listening conversations to solve problems and legitimize concerns.

The Ashton Unified School District

The superintendent, school leaders, members of the school board, and teachers realized the need for a new reading curriculum and approach for grades K–5. Ashton leaders were well-intentioned in their efforts and selected a quality reading program. The Ashton Unified School District is certainly a bigger enterprise than Kingsport City Schools; but surprisingly, the same effective communication needs were virtually identical in both. In thinking about overall communication, or that "free flow of meaning between people," three issues plagued their efforts.

The first issue was coordination of that communication. Because it is a relatively large district, there was a need to ensure that the *what* of this new reading program was well understood by all who were going to be talking about it. This group of communicators included the superintendent, district leaders, school leaders, and instructional coaches.

For example, instructional coaches were being brought into new roles themselves and had their hands full with just understanding their roles in schools, much less understanding a new content area. Explains Diane Connelly, "Coaches had been added in 2017–2018, and over time they became 'almost reading coaches,' working on just the reading implementation. Originally, coaches were not to be subject specific; they should be job-embedded colleagues. But the implementation of the coaches did not look that way. This added to the problem and the lack of trust teachers had in coaches. Tensions grew among the coaches and the teachers. It felt like pitting members against members."

Instructional coaches, then, were not all on the same page in their individual understanding of the new reading program. Similarly, some district leaders had great clarity about the new reading program, and some district leaders did not. To make matters a little more challenging, the curriculum and instruction division operated in relative isolation from the area directors of elementary schools (two different divisions). Those elementary directors relied on their own knowledge of the reading program to coach and counsel the principals they supervised. Because there was no coordinated effort and consistency of communication

(Continued)

(Continued)

between these two divisions, teachers and principals generally suffered. "We get the sense that the right hand and the left hand are not talking. Or the right hand and the left hand disagree. The messaging is not good," explains Conner Austen, AEA representative.

A second communication issue regarded the perceived lack of listening by district leaders. For instance, a teacher committee formed by the district leadership to examine the adopted reading program recommended, early in the initiation of the program, that the required preassessment listed in the program not be used. They felt that the transition from the old reading program to the new one would show misleading gaps of learning in students. The district, however, supported the wholesale use of the preassessment, to disastrous results. "There was an assessment that the K–2 teachers thought was a bad idea because the kids weren't ready for it," relates Conner Austen. "Teachers rallied at Ashton Unified School District board meetings and participated in public testimony, but it wasn't until an e-mail writing campaign where teachers voiced concerns to the Ashton Unified board that the assessment was pulled." In addition, there were early general concerns voiced by teachers in collective voice. Those concerns included the lack of perceived flexibility in delivery, inadequate reading materials for students, and a feeling that district leadership was trying to "inspect" quality into the new delivery of the program through frequent classroom visits (perceived by teachers as threatening or punitive) by both instructional coaches and principals. Again, the district leaders were unable to get their hands consistently around these issues, and communication was not coordinated in a way to reassure teachers.

A third issue was in the choice of language that was used to communicate about the reading program change. In almost all cases, the wording from district communication came from district leaders, not teachers or teacher representatives. The development of the Priority Plans illustrates how the *language* of the plans got the district into more deep water. District leaders thought the plans were perfectly clear in helping teachers see the flexibility in the new curriculum. Yet, because the "voice" in the plans felt like a leader voice, it was misinterpreted. Joanie Kemper shares one example of this: "We should have brought in teachers from non-Title schools for their input [on the Priority Plans] so there was a lens for those kids as well. Then schools could choose the model in the plans, depending on their school and what the students needed."

The resolution in some of the implementation issues was broadly detailed in an agreement that was hammered out by district leaders and local union representatives. In one section of that document, a statement identifies the type and level of collaboration that must exist between teachers and district leaders when selecting a new subject curriculum. While at the time of this publication this document is supposed to be the benchmark that guides future communication and decision-making, there is a nagging perception that the district is simply ignoring it. "As of today, the district has basically ignored the 450 language (the identifier for that portion of the agreement) that addresses collaboration, explains Austen. "[The local union] is fighting for the language in a current grievance. It seems the district doesn't 'share' that language with directors, and changes have been made after the language was agreed upon and the process in 450 was not followed."

Do the difficulties that Ashton has experienced seem insurmountable? You may be thinking that, but district leaders have not given up on effectively steering the reading program change. As of this publication date, there are actions that hopefully have had a positive impact on the implementation of the program:

- In the spring of 2019, the district and the local union sponsored a joint survey that examined teacher perceptions regarding the new reading program. The results of this survey were shared with all teachers and served as one guiding document as leaders sought to solve the problems with the program.

- District leaders (led by Joanie Kemper) and union representatives publish a regular communique to all teachers regarding what the district is doing to resolve issues and clarifying the intent of some reading decisions.

- The Priority Plans have undergone serious editing and reformatting by a teacher-led task force. Flexibility in instruction and program components have been emphasized in the plans, so teachers have more clarity as to the "negotiables and non-negotiables."

- The district leaders have committed to an overall assessment of the reading program. Data sources include teachers, principals,

(Continued)

(Continued)

instructional coaches, and students. The results of this analysis (three times a year) drive any improvements or adjustments to the program.

- Training with instructional coaches and principals has continued and has intensified in order to predict a certain level of reading knowledge and instructional understanding.

- There is more frequent and useful communication between the curriculum and instruction division and the elementary schools division.

The Ashton story is both a painful and useful one. On the one hand, it points out how quickly a change can crumble because of faulty initiation planning and lack of perceived coordination. On the other hand, it illustrates how persistence, strategy, and clear communication may help enliven a change on life support. The Ashton leaders were eager to hear a different point of view about the ways they were leading the change, and they were quite receptive to an outside source (me) looking in and giving consulting advice. One of their challenges may have been that they were a large district leadership staff who regularly operated in misaligned decision-making silos. Another challenge may have been the attempt to select one reading program to address a rather wide variety of students, abilities, and experiences. Several Ashton leaders talked to me about the independent streak that building leaders have always sought and enjoyed. Conformity to one reading program and more instructional boundaries may not have been their cup of tea. For whatever combination of reasons, the district is a great example of how leaders can continue to work at reconciling the need for personal independence with the need for consistency. It also gives us insights about how hard it is to make adjustments in implementation when emotional responses to the change are overwhelming planning and execution.

CHAPTER 8

FINDING THE MOMENTS

I once contracted full time with a large urban district in north Texas and spent three years as the "special assistant to the superintendent," training and coaching several hundred principals. My charge was to help principals become more focused and more intentional in their work. I remember one middle school principal well—a young man with lots of talent and skill—and every time I coached him, he always wanted to spend a lot of our time telling me *all* of the things he had done that day. He seemed to equate his level of "busy-ness" to leadership impact. Sound familiar?

This principal was a great guy who had the same chronic illness that many of us have—so wound up in his frantic blender of change that every day was a struggle to remember what he was really after. He was certainly "in the moment," but his moments were jumbled and without strategy. Even though his efforts were well-intentioned, he was running the risk of building change efforts that were almost guaranteed not to last. In fact, his own actions were contributing to the fragmented feeling his teachers were probably experiencing—and virtually no one in his school, the principal included, found joy or relevance in their daily work.

It didn't—and it doesn't—have to be that way. Greg McKeown, in his book *Essentialism: The Disciplined Pursuit of Less* (2014), offers an alternate way to lead, suggesting that it isn't the idea of saying "no" to more things, trimming your in-box, or learning a new time management strategy.

> It is about pausing constantly to ask, "Am I investing in the *right* activities?" There are far more activities and opportunities in the world than we have time and resources to invest in. And although many of them may be good, or even very good, the fact is that most are trivial and few are vital. The way of the Essentialist involves learning to tell the difference—learning to filter through all those options and selecting only those that are truly essential. (p. 5)

This is the kind of leadership that I find gives me joy—in that moment, to know what I'm doing and why I'm doing it. To act on knowledge of how people with whom I work respond and to create a culture that people love and can't bear the thought of leaving. To be transparent and yes, vulnerable to my own failings while learning from them.

In this book, I suppose we have taken an essentialist approach to school change. For us, the essential actions that McKeown suggests are in the context of the phase of change we are experiencing. A central theme of this book has been that the effective leader layers those daily moments within his or her own realization of and reflection on the phase of the change and what appears to be critical *at this time* in leading the change.

I have tried to write this book in a way that feels like you and I are having a conversation about the work. My illustrations of our two school districts have been written as two ongoing sagas. In the first few chapters, we looked at five critical/essential actions that will help guide your work at the beginning of the change, in the middle of the change, or when you are working to institutionalize the change.

You may not remember all of the information in this book, but hopefully you will remember and incorporate those five essential actions in your daily moments:

- Clarifying the purpose and messaging it with others
- Empathetically listening to all of your colleague's responses to the change
- Finding pathways for all of your colleagues to continue to get better at their craft
- Building trust in the work and in each other

- Facilitating a sense of real accomplishment among the people doing the work

In this concluding chapter, I won't give you more actions to take—I have made the case that those five actions are keys—and if we will all be focused on those actions, our changes will be more successful.

In addition to those five critical actions, I have also been realistic about resistance—the nagging feeling that some people aren't on board and the leadership dilemmas that feeling invokes. The approach we have taken is that resistance is almost inevitable and often arises because the leader doesn't pause during his or her moments and considers the realities of the change life span. Here, we have connected that life span of change and resistance—supporting the idea that resistance happens for a reason and it is often easily understood if we will take the time to do so.

I feel so strongly that we *can* (and really must) do a lot to lead and manage change more effectively. Well-known authors have been writing about effective school change for years. This book, however, has been an attempt to put it all together for each of us and to illustrate how peoples' responses to perceptions of change are not created in isolation—those perceptions are connected to the life of the change and what they may be feeling or needing.

> We *can* (and really must) do a lot to lead and manage change more effectively.

I plan to have the following intentions as I continue my work. These are personal for me, and I suspect they will have value for you. These personal intentions get at the morality of our work and the kind of fulfillment that we all want to share with the folks who come to work with us every day.

Get in Control

We lead the work—the work doesn't lead us. Grab hold of the work and be fearless in seizing the right combination of actions that you know will make things better for your teachers and students. Gain confidence in asking hard questions of your supervisors and those whom you supervise. Champion the "right" way to do things, and do not succumb, because of your own fatigue, to methods you know will yield inferior results.

Give Up to Gain

The hardest thing for me to do is to sometimes purposefully lose control of the situation. I have to realize that there are lots of folks who can make superior decisions. The issue for me has sometimes been that I haven't led in ways to nurture and cultivate that deep pool of talent. Listen to others, therefore, because they often have great ideas that were out of your personal box of strategies. Transparently admit your missteps; you will gain the respect and trust of your colleagues in ways you might not have imagined.

Take Your Time

Over and over, we have talked about the fact that real, sustained, lasting change takes time to take hold. Quick, sporadic efforts to change practices almost always result in failure and a negative mindset toward promising new ideas. Fight for the proper initiation of your change and find ways to report progress to your supervisors that allow the change to methodically take hold.

Dive Into the Resistance

Adopt my friend Rick DuFour's philosophy, which was to lean into the resistance as a way of "hearing" your colleagues' deepest fears around the change. Take time (there is that intention again!) to learn the possible reasons behind the resistance and then respond to it in a way that builds trust, develops the relationship, but doesn't deter from the result.

Build for Joy

Our unfocused, fragmented efforts do not create joy in our lives, our teachers' lives, or our students' lives. Joy is built from a community of purpose, communication, accomplishment, and appreciation of others. Find time to point out the small victories. Notice the efforts of your colleagues at work. Look them in the eyes and demonstrate your admiration for their effort. These are ways to build the deep love for work that we all seek.

My premise in all of these pages is that things can work much better. Our two districts were wonderful examples of unvarnished efforts—some of the efforts worked, and some didn't. What was admirable was the fact that their desire to do things better never wavered. Failures are simply hiccups in the process. Change can be built to last. We have known how to do it for years. I only hope that our work together serves as your handbook to find your moments.

References

Abrams, J. (2009). *Having hard conversations.* Thousand Oaks, CA: Corwin.

Ammabile, T., & Kramer, S. (2011). *The progress principle: Using small wins to ignite joy, engagement and creativity at work.* Boston, MA: Harvard Business Review Press.

Ariely, D. (2008). *Predictably irrational: The hidden forces that shape our decisions.* New York, NY: Harper-Collins.

Bechtle, M. (2012). *People can't drive you crazy if you don't give them the keys.* Grand Rapids, MI: Revel Publications.

Berger, W. (2014). *A more beautiful question.* New York, NY: Bloomsbury.

Bolman, L. G., & Deal, T. E. (2008). *Reframing organizations: Artistry, choice, & leadership* (4th ed.). San Francisco, CA: Jossey-Bass.

Bossidy, L., & Charan, R. (2009). *Execution: The discipline of getting things done.* New York, NY: Crown Publishing Group.

Brown, B. (2017). *Braving the wilderness: The quest for true belonging and the courage to stand alone.* New York, NY: Random House.

Cheliotes, L., & Reilly, M. (2010). *Coaching conversations: Transforming your school one conversation at a time.* Thousand Oaks, CA: Corwin.

Croft, A., Coggshall, J. G., Dolan, M., & Powers, E. (with Killion, J.). (2010). *Job-embedded professional development: What it is, who is responsible, and how to get it done well* (Issue Brief).

Washington, DC: National Comprehensive Center for Teacher Quality.

Danielson, C. (2009). *Talk about teaching.* Thousand Oaks, CA: Corwin.

Dweck, C. (2006). *Mindset: The new psychology of success.* New York, NY: Ballantine Books.

Ellis, D. (2009). *How to hug a porcupine.* New York, NY: Hatherleigh Press.

Farina, C., & Kotch, L. (2014). *A school leader's guide to excellence: Collaborating our way to better schools.* Portsmouth, NH: Heinemann.

Fullan, M. (2001). *Leading in a culture of change.* San Francisco, CA: Jossey-Bass.

Fullan, M. (2007). *The new meaning of educational change* (4th ed.). New York, NY: Teachers College Press.

Fullan, M. (2008). *The six secrets of change: What the best leaders do to help their organizations survive and thrive.* San Francisco, CA: Jossey-Bass.

Hall, G., & Hord, S. (2001). *Implementing change: Patterns, principles, and potholes.* Boston, MA: Allyn & Bacon.

Hargreaves, A., & Fullan, M. (2012). *Professional capital: Transforming teaching in every school.* New York, NY: Teachers College Press.

Harley, S. (2013). *How to say anything to anyone: A guide to building business relationships that really work.* Austin, TX: Greenleaf Book Group Press.

Hawley, W., & Valli, L. (1999). The essentials of effective professional development: A new consensus. In L. Darling-Hammond & G. Sykes (Eds.), *Teaching as the learning professional: A handbook of policy and practice* (pp. 127–150). San Francisco, CA: Jossey-Bass.

Hirsh, S., Psencik, K., & Brown, F. (2014). *Becoming a learning system.* Oxford, OH: Learning Forward.

Hord, S., & Roussin, J. (2013). *Implementing change through learning: Concerns-based concepts, tools, and strategies for guiding change.* Thousand Oaks, CA: Corwin.

Huberman, A., & Miles, M. (1984). *Innovation up close: How school improvement works.* New York, NY: Plenum Press.

Joyce, B., & Showers, B. (2003). Student achievement through staff development. National College for School Leadership. https://www .unrwa.org/sites/default/files/joyce_and_showers _coaching_as_cpd.pdf

Kahane, A. (2017). *Collaborating with the enemy: How to work with people you don't agree with or like or trust.* Oakland, CA: Berrett-Koehler.

Kaminski, J. (2011). Theory applied to informatics: Lewin's change theory. *CJNI: Canadian Journal of Nursing Informatics, 6*(1). Retrieved from http:// cjni.net/journal/?p=1210

Kegan, R., & Lahey, L. (2009). *Immunity to change: How to overcome it and unlock the potential in yourself and your organization.* Boston, MA: Harvard Business Review Press.

Knight, J. (2011). *Unmistakable impact: A partnership approach for dramatically improving instruction.* Thousand Oaks, CA: Corwin.

Kotter, J. (2012). *Leading change.* Boston, MA: Harvard Business Review Press.

Lawrence, P. (1969, January). How to deal with resistance to change. *Harvard Business Review.* Retrieved from https://hbr.org/1969/01/how-to- deal-with-resistance-to-change

Lazare, A. (2004). *On apology.* New York, NY: Oxford University Press.

Little, J. (2008). Declaration of interdependence. *Journal of Staff Development, 29*(3), 53–56.

Masterson, M. (2008). *Ready, fire, aim: Zero to $100 million in no time flat.* New York, NY: Wiley.

McKeown, G. (2014). *Essentialism: The disciplined pursuit of less.* New York, NY: Crown Business.

Meyerson, D. E. (2001). *Tempered radicals: How people use difference to inspire change at work.* Boston, MA: Harvard Business School Press.

Patterson, K., Grenny, J., McMillan, R., & Switzler, A. (2002). *Crucial conversations: Tools for talking when stakes are high.* New York, NY: McGraw-Hill.

Patterson, K., Grenny, J., Maxfield, D., McMillan, R., & Switzler, A. (2013). *Crucial accountability: Tools for resolving violated expectations, broken commitments, and bad behavior* (2nd ed.). New York, NY: McGraw-Hill.

Pearson, P. D., & Gallagher, G. (1983). The gradual release of responsibility model of instruction. *Contemporary Educational Psychology, 8,* 112–123.

Pink, D. (2009). *Drive: The surprising truth about what motivates us.* New York, NY: Riverhead Books.

Powell, W., & Kusuma-Powell, O. (2015). Overcoming resistance to new ideas. *Phi Delta Kappan, 96*(8), 66–69.

Re-evaluating incremental innovation. (2018, September/October). *Harvard Business Review.* Retrieved from https://hbr.org/2018/09/ reevaluating-incremental-innovation

Reeves, D., & Eaker, R. (2019). *100-day leaders: Turning short-term wins into long-term success in schools.* Bloomington, IN: Solution Tree.

Sergiovanni, T. (1992). *Moral leadership; Getting to the heart of school improvement.* San Francisco, CA: Jossey-Bass.

Shapiro, A. B. (2011, August 10). Learning with our friends: The zone of proximal development. *Psychology Today.* Retrieved from https://www.psychologytoday.com/blog/healing-possibility/201108/learning-our-friends-the-zone-proximal-development

Sinek, S. (2009). *Start with why: How great leaders inspire everyone to take action.* New York, NY: Penguin Group.

Stanier, M. B. (2016). *The coaching habit: Say less, ask more, & change the way you lead forever.* Toronto, CA: Box of Crayons Press.

Stone, D., & Heen, S. (2014). *Thanks for the feedback: The science and art of receiving feedback well.* New York, NY: Viking Press.

Tannen, D. (1998). *The argument culture: Stopping America's war of words.* New York, NY: Ballantine Books.

Texas Leadership Center. (1999). *The leadership development process.* Austin, TX: Texas Leadership Center.

Tomlinson, C., & Murphy, M. (2015). *Leading for differentiation: Growing teachers who grow kids.* Alexandria, VA: ASCD.

Tomlinson, C., & Murphy, M. (2018). The empathetic school. *Educational Leadership, 75*(6), 20–27.

Tschannen-Moran, M. (2004). *Trust matters: Leadership for successful schools.* San Francisco, CA: Jossey-Bass.

Tschannen-Moran, M., & Tschannen-Moran, B. (2010). *Evocative coaching: Transforming schools one conversation at a time.* San Francisco, CA: Jossey-Bass.

Vygotsky, L. (1980). *Mind in society.* Boston, MA: Harvard University Press.

Vygotsky, L. (1986). *Thought and language* (2nd ed.). Boston, MA: MIT Press.

Walsh, J., & Sattes, B. (2010). *Leading through quality questioning: Creating capacity, commitment, and community.* Thousand Oaks, CA: Corwin.

Zak, P. (2017). *Trust factor: The science of creating high-performance companies.* New York, NY: Amacom.

Zuckoff, A., & Gorscak, B. (2015). Finding your way to change: How the power of motivational interviewing can reveal what you want and help you get there. New York, NY: Guilford Press.

Index

A SAGE Publishing Company

Helping educators make the greatest impact

CORWIN HAS ONE MISSION: to enhance education through intentional professional learning.

We build long-term relationships with our authors, educators, clients, and associations who partner with us to develop and continuously improve the best evidence-based practices that establish and support lifelong learning.

Leadership That Makes an Impact

MICHAEL FULLAN & MARY JEAN GALLAGHER

With the goal of transforming the culture of learning to develop greater equity, excellence, and student well-being, this book will help you liberate the system and maintain focus.

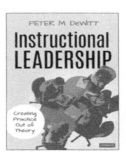

PETER M. DEWITT

This step-by-step how-to guide presents the six driving forces of instructional leadership within a multistage model for implementation, delivering lasting improvement through small collaborative changes.

BRYAN GOODWIN

If you've ever wondered anything, really—just out of curiosity—then you have what it takes to lead your school to restored curiosity and your students to well-being and success.

JOHN HATTIE & RAYMOND L. SMITH

Based on the most current Visible Learning® research with contributions from education thought leaders around the world, this book includes practical ideas for leaders to implement high-impact strategies to strengthen entire school cultures and advocate for all students.

DAVIS CAMPBELL & MICHAEL FULLAN

The model outlined in this book develops a systems approach to governing local schools collaboratively to become exemplars of highly effective decision-making, leadership, and action.

MICHAEL FULLAN, JOANNE QUINN, & JOANNE MCEACHEN

The comprehensive strategy of deep learning incorporates practical tools and processes to engage educational stakeholders in new partnerships, mobilize whole-system change, and transform learning for all students.

JOANNE QUINN, JOANNE MCEACHEN, MICHAEL FULLAN, MAG GARDNER, & MAX DRUMMY

Dive into deep learning with this hands-on guide to creating learning experiences that give purpose, unleash student potential, and transform not only learning, but life itself.

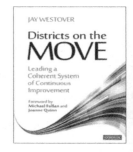

JAY WESTOVER

The transformative framework outlined in this book creates a districtwide approach for changing the culture of learning and creating a coherent system of continuous improvement.

ANTHONY KIM, KEARA MASCARENAZ, & KAWAI LAI

This guide provides battle-tested practices to help leaders build better habits for team learning, meetings, and projects, to achieve a more responsive, innovative organization.

EVAN ROBB

Build the foundations of effective leadership despite daily distractions. Learn how to intentionally use ten-minute opportunities to consider and execute your vision.

AMY TEPPER & PATRICK FLYNN

Nineteen strategies help leaders, coaches, and teachers improve their ability to identify desired outcomes, recognize learning in action, collect relevant evidence, and develop effective feedback.

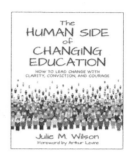

JULIE M. WILSON

Learn to make sense of challenging change journeys and accelerate implementation with this practical framework that includes human-centered tools, resources, and mini case studies.

GRANT LICHTMAN

Our rapidly evolving world is dramatically impacting how we view schools. *Thrive* shows educators how they can help their schools not only survive but thrive during rapid change.

ERIC SHENINGER

The future-forward framework in this book prepares leaders to harness the power of innovative ideas and digital strategies to create relevant, engaging, and intuitive school cultures.

CHRISTINE MASON, PAUL LIABENOW, & MELISSA PATSCHKE

Envision and enact transformative change with an iterative visioning process, thought-provoking vignettes, case studies from exemplary schools, key strategies and tools, and practical implementation ideas.

KIRSTEN RICHERT, JEFFREY IKLER, & MARGARET ZACCHEI

Shifting empowers educational change leaders to proactively and coherently navigate complex, unprecedented change in schools and establish a school culture in which changemakers can thrive.

Made in the USA
Monee, IL
25 August 2021